CISSP

2 Books in 1:

The Complete Beginner's Guide to Learn the Fundamentals of Information System Security

+

Tips and Strategies to Pass the CISSP Exam on Your First Attempt

© Copyright 2020 by Robert Preston
All rights reserved.

This document is geared towards providing exact and reliable information with regards to the topic and issue covered. The publication is sold with the idea that the publisher is not required to render accounting, officially permitted, or otherwise, qualified services. If advice is necessary, legal or professional, a practiced individual in the profession should be ordered.

From a Declaration of Principles which was accepted and approved equally by a Committee of the American Bar Association and a Committee of Publishers and Associations.

In no way is it legal to reproduce, duplicate, or transmit any part of this document in either electronic means or in printed format. Recording of this publication is strictly prohibited and any storage of this document is not allowed unless with written permission from the publisher. All rights reserved.

The information provided herein is stated to be truthful and consistent, in that any liability, in terms of inattention or otherwise, by any usage or abuse of any policies, processes, or directions contained within is the solitary and utter responsibility of the recipient reader. Under no circumstances will any legal responsibility or blame be held against the publisher for any reparation, damages, or monetary loss due to the information herein, either directly or indirectly.

Respective authors own all copyrights not held by the publisher.

The information herein is offered for informational purposes solely, and is universal as so. The presentation of the information is without contract or any type of guarantee assurance.

The trademarks that are used are without any consent, and the publication of the trademark is without permission or backing by the trademark0 owner. All trademarks and brands within this book are for clarifying purposes only and are the owned by the owners themselves, not affiliated with this document.

Table of Contents

INTRODUCTION TO CISSP 7

CHAPTER ONE SECURITY AND RISK MANAGEMENT 16

CHAPTER TWO ASSETS SECURITY 56

CHAPTER THREE SECURITY ARCHITECTURE AND ENGINEERING 72

CHAPTER FOUR COMMUNICATION AND NETWORK SECURITY 83

CHAPTER FIVE IDENTIFY AND ACCESS MANAGEMENT 100

CHAPTER SIX SECURITY ASSESSMENT AND TESTING 117

CHAPTER SEVEN SECURITY OPERATIONS 135

CHAPTER EIGHT SOFTWARE DEVELOPMENT SECURITY 145

CISSP: TIPS AND STRATEGIES

CISSP REQUIREMENTS 157
CISSP EXAM STRUCTURE 161
CISSP EXAM RULES 166
CISSP 8 DOMAINS 170
HOW TO PLAN YOUR STUDY FOR CISSP 175
30 DAYS STUDY PLAN 186
WHY YOU NEED TO JOIN A STUDY GROUP 192
CISSP TRAINING SEMINARS 197
WHO MUST DO A CISSP COURSE? 198
WHERE TO STUDY AND WHY IT'S IMPORTANT TO USE MULTIPLE SOURCES 199
HOW TO PRACTICE WITH PAST QUESTIONS AND WHERE TO FIND THEM 203
HOW TO MANAGE YOUR TIME DURING EXAMS 209
THE SPECIFIC TERMS OF CISSP, THE MOST COMMONLY USED TERMS AND THEIR MEANING 212
TIPS AND TRICKS TO PASS THE EXAM 244
HOW TO APPROACH DIFFICULT CISSP EXAM QUESTIONS 246
CISSP TOPICS AND RESOURCES 250

INTRODUCTION TO CISSP

The CISSP Program covers subject matter in many different Information Security subjects. The CISSP examination is dependent on exactly what (ISC)² conditions the frequent Body of Knowledge (or CBK). In accordance with (ISC)², that the CISSP CBK is a taxonomy - a group of subjects related to information security professionals across the globe.

CISSP Certification or Licensed Information Systems Security Professional credential is an advanced and gruelling evaluation that assesses the abilities of information security specialists and confirms their own skills to secure a company atmosphere. Becoming a CISSP accredited practitioner is not a cakewalk. It requires years of related job experience in addition to an endorsement by a current CISSP specialist to opt for the 6-hour long-term exam. The exam is conducted by (ISC)2 and provides vendor-neutral capabilities applicable internationally and industry-wide.

The industry is overwhelmed by a broad selection of information security certificates and (ISC)2 CISSP certification have become one of the top IT security certification and tons of organizations seek employees with this certification for both IT jobs and managerial positions. This certification facilitates an IT security specialist's dedication and several years of expertise in the profession. The excellent thing about this is that organizations are always looking for skilled IT security specialists with this particular qualification.

Despite having over 70,000 active CISSP experts around the globe organizations are searching for more, this underscores the industry need. Certification is generally a part of professional improvement and companies provide rewards to people that get them. According to (ISC)2, there is a demand for two (two) million CISSP specialists for the subsequent three (3) years to match the increasing requirement.

Prerequisites

· Have a minimum of five years of direct full-time safety work experience in a couple of the (ISC)² data security domains (CBK). 1 year can be waived for having a four-year school diploma, a master's degree in Information security, or for owning one of a range of different certificates. A candidate with no five years of experience may make the associate of (ISC)² designation bypassing the necessary CISSP evaluation, valid for a maximum of six years. During these six years, the candidate will have to acquire the essential 5 years expertise and submit the mandatory endorsement form for the certificate for a CISSP. Upon completion of the professional experience demands the certificate is going to be converted into CISSP status.

· Attest to the fact of the assertions regarding skilled experience and take the CISSP Code of Ethics.

· Response questions concerning the criminal history and related background.

· Pass the multiple choice CISSP examinations with a scaled score of 700 points or higher from 1000 possible points.

· Have their credentials endorsed by a different (ISC)² certificate holder in a good position.

(ISC)2, that produced and retains the CISSP eligibility, upgraded the arrangement of the certificate in 2015, moving from ten domains.

By 15 April 2018, the CISSP program is updated as follows:

1) Security and Risk Control

Risk and Safety Management comprises roughly 15% of the CISSP examination.

This Is the largest domain in CISSP, offering a comprehensive breakdown of those scenarios that you wish to know about data systems management. It covers:

- The confidentiality, integrity, and accessibility of information;
- Safety Management fundamentals;
- Compliance needs;
- Legal and regulatory issues pertaining to information protection;
- IT policies and procedures; and
- Risk-based management concepts.

2) Asset Security

Asset Security comprises about 10 percentage of the CISSP examination.

This domain Addresses the physical essentials of data security. It covers:

- The classification and ownership of resources and data;
- Privacy;
- Retention periods;
- Data security controls; and
- handling demands.

3) Security Architecture and Engineering

Safety Engineering comprises about 13 percentage of the CISSP examination.

This domain Covers several significant data security theories, for example:

- Engineering procedures using secure design principles;
- Fundamental theories of security variations;
- Safety capabilities of information technology;
- Assessing and mitigating vulnerabilities in programs;
- Cryptography; and

- Designing and executing physical security.

4) Communications and Network Security

Communications And Network Security Comprises about 14% of the CISSP examination.

This domain Covers the design and protection of their organization's approaches. Including:

- Safe design principles for neighbourhood design;

- Safe network components; and

- Secure communication channels.

5) Access and Access Control

Identity and Access Control Includes about 13% of the CISSP examination.

This domain helps data safety professionals understand how to control how users may get information. It covers:

- Physical and logical access to sources;

- Identification and authentication;

- Integrating identity to get a ceremony and third party identity alternatives;

- Authorisation mechanics; and

- The identification and access provisioning lifecycle.

6) Security Assessment and Testing

Safety Assessment and Testing comprise about 12% of the CISSP examination.

This domain focuses on the design, performance, and analysis of security testing. It comprises:

- Designing and supporting assessment and analysis plans;
- Security management testing;
- Collecting security process information;
- Assessment Cards;
- Internal and third-party security instructions.

7) Security Operations

Safety Operations comprises about 13 Percentage of the CISSP examination.

This domain name summarizes how plans are put to actions. It covers:

- Recognizing and supporting investigations;
- Prerequisites for analysis types;
- Logging and monitoring actions;
- Securing the source of resources;
- Foundational security operations ideas;

- Implementing resource safety methods;
- Incident management;
- Disaster recovery;
- Managing physical security; and
- Business continuity.

8) Software Development Security

Software Development Security Comprises about 10% of the CISSP exam.

This domain helps professionals to understand, apply and apply software security. It covers:

- Security in the software development life cycle;
- Safety controls in expansion surroundings;
- The Efficacy of software security; and
- Safe programming guidelines and standards.
- CISSP revision and training stuff

Individuals who sit the CISSP CBK (Common Body of Knowledge) evaluation will be examined on each of the eight domains.

The examination comprises 250 multiple-choice inquiries and lasts 6 hours. The passing grade is 70%.

Specializations in CISSP Certification

• Management (CISSP-ISSMP) • Architecture (CISSP-ISSAP) • Engineering (CISSP-ISSEP)

Skills Shortage

Job openings for IT security areas frequently record CISSP certificate as one of those pre-requisites. Other cyber security certificates in demand include CEH, CHFI, and Cisco Security credentials. It is a compulsory requirement especially in the case of banks, insurance companies and other financial institutions where the cost of a data breach is relatively important. The need for fantastic and knowledgeable security experts is within an all-time big and assorted research is pointing at a scarcity of cyber protection skills. At this time, it gets much more crucial to acquire certification and reinforce your position in the data protection industry.

Compensation of CISSP at the business

According to current occupation and livelihood sites, the standard salary for a CISSP expert fluctuates between $60K to $140K. Unexpectedly CISSP professionals earn 20 percent over the non CISSPs. Work experience is also a vital aspect taken into consideration when determining reimbursement. It generally needs a work adventure of ten (10) years or longer for experts to make the desired six (6) figure income. This also depends upon the form of industry employing. Typically you may locate a $14K variance involving the accredited compared to some non-certified and 10 percent, 20 percent on a global average. Besides the employability benefits, CISSPs emerge as affiliates of a distinctive group. It's observed that primary cities such as San Francisco in addition to Chicago in the majority of cases provide greater reimbursement.

CISSP like any other certificates has been a casualty of review. Despite all the analysis and recommended choices, it's lasted the test of time and remains the certification for information security specialists.

Benefits of Being Accredited

Now, let's know how the CISSP certification will help. Originally, it frees you as a valid IT security expert. It raises your reputation and credentials. It'll get you beyond the pre-screening process and qualifies you for the subsequent round of interviews. Fundamentally, the CISSP certificate offers you an edge over rivals. The demand for cyber security specialists continues to grow due to increasing computer dangers. IT security might well be one of the few markets in which chance is ample and therefore fulfilling. There's an enormous small number of seasoned professionals. There's unquestionably a fantastic demand for IT security specialists within the upcoming few years with the progress in technology.

CHAPTER ONE
SECURITY AND RISK MANAGEMENT

INTRODUCTION

Computing technology Isn't confined to mainframes and PCs anymore. Both simple and innovative devices are now a part of our daily lives, which range from road signs to smart vending machines to innovative diagnosing health care services. Every one of those new kinds of apparatus has to be procured since all of them have their particular requirements concerning Confidentiality, Integrity, and access to the resources or data they supply.

Risk management entails comprehensive comprehension, analysis, and risk-mitigating strategies to determine that organizations attain their data security goal. Risk is basically inherent in every facet of data security choice and so risk management theories aid assist each choice to work in character.

The significant components of Safety and Risk Management essential for CISSP include:

- Information safety inside the company / Security Model
- The triad of data security -- Confidentiality, Integrity, and Availability
- Safety governance fundamentals
- Business continuity requirements
- Policies, criteria, processes, and guidelines
- Risk management theories
- Threat simulating

Aims of a Safety Model

The two main objectives of Data security within the business by a risk management standpoint include:

- Have controls set up to support the mission of their organization?
- Each of the choices ought to be based on the risk tolerance of company, benefit, and cost.

Willing to take your skills into the following level? Consider registering for a hands-on CISSP course. Complete the form below for InfoSec Institute's boot camp prices.

Plan Contributes to Tactics; Approaches directly to Operations.

Operational targets may include patching computers as required, encouraging users, upgrading anti-virus signatures, and keeping the total system on a daily basis. Corresponding strategic goals could involve transferring computers into domain names, installing firewalls, and segregating the system by making a demilitarized zone. Afterward, the tactical aims may refer to using all domains professionally administered and implementing VPNs and RADIUS servers to make available an extremely secure environment which gives a fantastic quantity of confidence to the management and personnel.

A safety model has distinct layers, but in addition, it has different kinds of goals to reach in various time frames. Daily aims, or operational objectives, concentrate on productivity and task-oriented activities to ensure the organization's performance in a smooth and predictable way. Mid-term objectives, or strategic objectives, could signify incorporating all workstations and tools into a single domain more fundamental control can be gained. A long-term aim, or tactical aim, may entail transferring all of the branches out of dedicated communication lines to frame relay, implementing IPsec virtual private networks (VPNs) for many remote users rather than dial-up entry, and incorporating wireless technologies together with the extensive security options and controls present inside the surroundings.

This technique and strategy to plan are known as the preparation horizon. A business can't typically execute all changes at the same time, and a few changes are bigger than others. Many times there appears a scenario wherein certain changes can't occur until some other modifications occur. When an organization whose system is presently decentralized, and operates in workgroups with no domain trust, needs to execute its own certification authority (CA) and public key infrastructure (PKI) business-wide, this cannot occur in a week's time. The operational aims are to maintain production running easy and make modest steps towards readying the surroundings for a domain name structure. The strategic goal is to place all workstations and tools to a domain and centralize access control and authentication. The strategic objective is to get all workstations, servers, and devices within the business to use the public infrastructure to provide authentication, encryption, and also extra secure communication stations.

Usually, security functions best if It is Operational, Tactical, and Strategic aims are described and operate to encourage each other. This could be more challenging than it seems.

Safety Basics

Confidentiality, ethics, and accessibility (that the CIA triad) is a normal security framework meant to guide policies for data security within a company.

1. Confidentiality: Avoid unauthorized disclosure

Confidentiality of data refers to protecting the data from disclosure to unauthorized parties.

Key areas for keeping Qualifications:

- Social Engineering: Training and consciousness, specifying Separation of Duties in the strategic level, enforcing policies and running Vulnerability Assessments
- Media Reuse: Suitable Sanitization Plans
- Eavesdropping: Utilization of encryption and maintaining sensitive data from the community with sufficient access controls

2. Coding: Detect Modification of info

The ethics of information denotes protecting sensitive data from being altered by unauthorized parties.

Key areas for keeping Confidentiality:

- Encryption -- design based calculations
- Intentional or Malicious Modification
    - Message Digest (Hash)
    - MAC
    - Digital Signatures

3. Availability: Supply timely And dependable access to sources

Access to information signifies Ensuring that all of the required or planned celebrations can get the data when required.

Key areas for keeping Accessibility:

- Avoid single point of collapse
- Comprehensive fault tolerance (Information, Hard Drives, Servers, Network Links, etc.)

Best Practices to Support CIA

Separation of Duties: Prevents any 1 individual from becoming too strong within a business. This coverage also supplies singleness of attention. As an example, a network administrator who's worried about providing users access to sources should not ever be the safety administrator. This coverage also helps stop collusion since there are lots of people with distinct skills. Separation of duties controls.

Wanted Vacations: Prevents an operator from having exclusive use of a method. Gradually, that person is made to take a holiday and relegate the constraint of the machine to somebody else. This coverage is a detective control.

Job spinning: Similar in function to compulsory holidays, but with the added plus of cross-training workers.

Least freedom: Allowing users to have just the essential accessibility to perform their jobs.

Have to understand: Along with clearance, users should also have "need to learn" to get classified data.

Double control: Requiring greater than 1 user to carry out a job.

Risk Control

Risk management is the process of identifying, analyzing, measuring, mitigating, or shifting risk. Its principal purpose is to lessen the likelihood or impact of an identified threat. The threat management lifecycle comprises all risk-related activities like Assessment, Analysis, Mitigation, and continuing Risk Tracking which we'll discuss at the latter portion of the report.

The achievement of a safety program can be traced to a comprehensive comprehension of danger. Without appropriate consideration and analysis of risks, the appropriate controllers might not be applied. Risk evaluation ensures that we identify and assess our resources, then identify dangers as well as their corresponding vulnerabilities.

Risk evaluation allows us to prioritize Those dangers and finally assign a dollar value to each threat event. Once we've got a dollar value for a specific risk, we could make an educated choice about which mitigation strategy best suits our requirements. And lastly, as with all elements of safety policy, continuing evaluation is indispensable. New attacks and other dangers are constantly emerging, and safety professionals must remain informed and current.

Risk -- Key points to know about

- Every choice begins by looking at danger.
- Ascertain the value of your resources.
- Assess and identify economical solutions to decrease risk to an acceptable degree (infrequently can we remove risk).

- Remember that Safeguards are proactive and Countermeasures are reactive.

The next definitions are crucial for hazard management:

- Asset: Anything of significance to the firm
- Vulnerability: A weakness; the lack of a shield
- Threat: Matters that may pose a threat to part or all of an advantage
- Threat Agent: The thing which carries out the assault
- Harness: A instance of undermine
- Risk: The likelihood of a hazard materializing
- Controls: Physical, Administrative and Technical Protections
    - Safeguards
    - Countermeasures

Multiple scenario-based use instances are Assessed in CISSP, depending on the following general resources of danger:

- Terrible, unpatched or non-existing anti-virus applications
- Disgruntled employees posing an inner hazard
- Poor physical safety controllers
- Bad access controls
- Lack of change management
- Lack of proper procedures for hardening systems
- Poorly trained customers and too little consciousness

This outline represents the Lifecycle of Risk Control

- Risk Assessment

- Categorize, Classify and Valuate Assets
- Know/Identify Hazards and Vulnerabilities
- Risk Evaluation
  - Qualitative
  - Quantitative
- Risk Mitigation/Response
  - Reduce/Avoid
  - Transport
  - Accept/Reject

Each segment within the lifecycle is critical for CISSP and has been further described below:

Risk Assessment:

Appears at dangers corresponding to recognized parameters for a particular period and have to be evaluated periodically. Managing risks is a continuous procedure.

The next measures are formally part of a Risk Assessment according to NIST 800-30:
- System Characterization
- Threat Identification
- Vulnerability Identification
- Control Evaluation
- Likelihood Determination
- Impact Evaluation
- Risk Determination
- Control Recommendation
- Results Documentation

Risk Analysis:

- Discovering a value for a hazard.
- Qualitative vs. Quantitative

- Qualitative analysis (subjective, judgment-based)
  - Subjective in nature
  - Software words such as "high, moderate,""non" to explain the likelihood and severity of the effect of a hazard exposing a vulnerability
- Quantitative Analysis (objective, figures driven)
  - More expertise required than with Qualitative
  - Involves calculations to Ascertain a dollar value associated with each hazard element
  - Business decisions are essentially driven by this kind of analysis.
    - More expertise required compared to Qualitative
    - Involves calculations to ascertain a dollar value associated with each hazard section
    - Business choices are basically driven by this kind of analysis.
    - Essential to get a cost/benefit evaluation
    - Crucial pointers to be recalled
      - AV -- Asset Value
      - EF -- Exposure Variable
      - ARO -- Annual Rate of Occurrence
      - Single Loss Expectancy = AV * EF
      - Annual Loss Expectancy = SLE*ARO
      - The price of management should be the Exact Same or less than the possibility of reduction.

- Risk Worth = Probability * Effect
- Probability: Just how likely is it to materialize the danger?
- Effect: What's the extent of harm?
  - It could also be known as chances and seriousness.

Mitigating Risk

- Three okay risk answers:
  - Reduce
  - Transport
  - Accept
- Continue to track for dangers
- The way we opt to mitigate business risks becomes the foundation for Safety Governance and Policy.

Security Governance

The objective of security governance would be to make sure that safety plans, aims, risks, and goals are evaluated based on some top-notch model. By doing this, we guarantee that those ultimately accountable for the failures or success of a safety system are involved.

To attain security governance, Security patterns need to be made to permit organizations to implement procedures and practices to encourage their safety objectives and the general mission of these associations. Various business consortiums have given insight into the aims, goals, and way of creating powerful Information Security Management Systems (ISMS).

The next industry standards are a number of those which offer multiple frameworks that may be assessed when generating security baselines to accomplish security governance.

> BS 7799, ISO 17799, and 27000 Series
> COBIT and COSO
> OCTAVE
> ITIL

Strategy to Security Management

Bad security direction triggers the Vast majority of an organization's safety issues. Security has to be guided and supported by top management, known as the top-notch approach since without this, any safety efforts will be doomed. Unfortunately, most firms follow a bottom-up approach, in which the IT department takes safety seriously and tries to develop a safety program. This strategy generally won't offer those people with the necessary funds, resources, support, or focus. Therefore, it's often doomed from the beginning.

Information Management Security Program mostly consists of the following key aspects to Know about:

- Functions and Duties
- Policies/Standards/Procedures/Guidelines
- SLA's Service Level Agreements/Outsourcing
- Data Classification/Security
- Auditing

Senior management's functions and responsibilities across these regions are usually assessed for CISSP and therefore are crucial for the total comprehension of the safety risk management for any business.

Development and Service of Policies: Senior management is responsible for the company-wide policies within a company. These policies must be high tech statements from the direction that detail the organization's philosophy and commitment to safety. Furthermore, it's the administration's responsibility to guarantee the enforcement of those policies, and also to lead by example.

Allocations of Resources: Senior management is responsible for supplying the required resources to Allow policies to be completed. A genuine comprehension of issues regarding liability is essential so as to warrant the resources.

Selections according to Risk: It's senior management's job to be the greatest decision-maker for your own organization. Once supplied with all the facts from a hazard analysis, it's up to management to make conclusions on types of Risk Mitigation.

Safety Policy: The company's safety policy is a high-tech record that contains generalized details of this administration's directive pertaining to safety's function within the company. It determines the way the safety program is going to be put up, dictates the program's aims, assigns responsibility, reveals the backdrop, and clarifies the tactical and strategic values of safety. It clarifies how authorities will be completed and address regulations and laws which it fulfils. It will offer direction and scope for all future actions within the business. Following the safety policy is defined, the next step would be producing the criteria, guidelines, processes, baselines, etc. The Safety Policy should always encourage the strategic goals of the company.

Domain Name 1 begins with info on the 3 pillars of Information Security - Confidentiality, Integrity, and Availability, describing the importance of each principle from the truth. Then, the Domain clarifies the gap between the information Security Management and Information Security Governance theories.

Next, the Domain describes the way to draft your information Security Goals as Strategic (long term), Tactical (six weeks to a year) and Operational (less than months) targets. The aims should be dependent on the safety goals derived from the company safety goals, also referred to as DUE CARE goals. The Domain clarifies the gap between "Due Care" goals and "Due Diligence" objectives.

The Domain offers advice on contents of an Information Security coverage and the way the coverage differs from a process, a benchmark, a baseline along with a principle document. Including the Comprehensive Comprehension of "Information Security" functions and duties for Senior Management, that the Chief Information Security Officer, that the Data Owner, that the Data Custodian, the System Owner, the System Administrator along with also the Security Administrator. The theories of the roles and obligations are analyzed quite a bit from the real CISSP Exam.

The Domain moves to describe different kinds of controllers (Administrative, Technical and Physical) and theories such as segregation of duties, job rotation, mandatory vacations, spilt knowledge and double control. Then, the Domain Name shares advice about Information Security clinics in hiring new workers and employee termination. Again, these theories are analyzed in the real CISSP Exam.

Since the title of the Domain Name implies -"Risk Management" - this domain name delves into describing the principles of Risk Control such as Assets (both tangible and intangible), Vulnerability, Threat, finishing a "Business Impact Analysis" practice and developing a hazard register. Thereafter, we know to comprehend the danger remediation approaches (Risk Mitigation, Risk Transfer, Risk Avoidance and Risk Acceptance).

We know The very popular Risk Control worldwide approaches such as Octave, ISO 27005 and NIST 800-30. Although these standards/risk control frameworks aren't vital for the CISSP examination, the anticipation is that we know them to a high degree, at least the titles.

Post-understanding The risk management theories, the Domain offers advice on Enterprise Architecture Frameworks such as Zachman, SABSA and TOGAF. The expectation is to comprehend those enterprise architecture frameworks in a definition degree and know-how one frame differs in another frame. Please refer to the attached Inspection Notes for more detail.

The Domain clarifies the concepts around Business Continuity Management (BCM). The main reason for such as the BCM theories is the methodology into developing a business continuity plan comes from hazard managing the business resources.

The following Subject from the Domain Name is Legal Laws, Categories of Legislation, theories around Proximate Causation, Exigent Circumstances, Prudent Man Rule, Data Protection Act, Privacy Laws, and Safe Harbour. The expectation is that you know these laws to a high degree.

The Domain defines the Intellectual Property Laws, Patents, Trademark, Copyright, and Trade Secrets. In Addition to this, we all learn the concepts around IT Forensics, chain of custody, forms of signs, computer surveillance and finally, the ISC2 Code of Ethics.

Risk is a vital part to our lives. In each action we intend to take in our private and professional lives, we must examine the dangers associated with that. From a cyber safety standpoint, businesses like energy, health care, banking, retail, retail, etc., involves a lot of dangers which impedes the adoption of technologies and that needs to be efficiently handled. The related risks that will need to be addressed evolve immediately and have to be managed in a brief time period.

The Certified Information Systems Security Professional (CISSP) is a Data security certificate that was designed from the International Information Systems Security Certification Consortium, also known as (ISC)², The threat management is just one of those modules of CISSP training which involves the identification of a company's information assets and the development, documentation, implementation, and updating of policies, criteria, processes, and guidelines which ensure confidentiality, integrity, and accessibility.

Management tools like hazard assessment and hazard analysis are Utilized to Identify threats, classify assets, and to speed up their vulnerabilities so that effective security measures and controls could be put into place. The practice of risk management is completed to determine possible dangers, practices, tools, speed and lessen the risk to certain resources of a company.

Risk Control Concepts

Beyond basic safety principles, the concepts of risk management are Possibly the most significant and complex area of the data security and threat management realm name. It's crucial for the candidate to comprehend all of the core concepts of hazard management like hazard assessment methods, risk calculations, and shield selection criteria and goals.

A risk includes a threat and a vulnerability of an advantage, defined as follows:

Threat: Any man-made or natural circumstance which may have a negative effect on an organizational advantage.

Vulnerability: The lack or weakness of a shield within an advantage which produces a threat potentially more likely to happen, or likely to happen more often.

Asset: An asset is a source, procedure, product, or system that's some significance to a company and must, therefore, be shielded.

The threat, vulnerability, and exemptions are known as hazard management triples. It's the major concept that's coated in risk management from the CISSP examination standpoint. Risk cannot be completely removed. Any system or surroundings, however secure, can become compromised.

Threat x ray = Risk

Some dangers or events, such as natural disasters are mostly inconsistent. As a result, the most important objective of risk management is risk mitigation that entails decreasing risk to a level that is acceptable to a company. There are 3 Chief components of that risk management is included of:

- Identification
- Evaluation
- Control

Risk identification:

Risk identification is the first step in the hazard management that entails Identifying certain elements of the 3 elements of risk: resources, threats, and vulnerabilities.

Asset valuation:

To ascertain the right degree of safety, the identification of a company's assets and ascertaining their worth is a crucial step. The worth of an asset to a company could be both qualitative (associated with its price) and qualitative (its relative significance).

Any incorrect asset evaluation may result in:

- Poorly selected or implemented controllers.
- Controls that are not cost-effective.
- Controls shield the Incorrect asset.

While a correctly conducted advantage evaluation procedure has several advantages to a company:

- Supports qualitative and qualitative risk assessments, business impact assessments, and safety auditing.

- Facilitates cost-benefit evaluation and supports management decisions concerning the choice of proper safeguards.
- May be used to determine insurance requirements, budgeting, and substitute expenses.
- Help show due care and limit liability.

There are 3 Chief elements which are utilised to ascertain the worth of assets:

First and upkeep prices: This is often a concrete dollar value and might involve buying, licensing, development, maintenance, and service costs.

Organizational value: This is often a hard and subjective value. It might include the expense of producing, acquiring, and re-creating info, and the company's impact or reduction if the data is compromised or lost.

Public worth: Public worth may consist of loss of proprietary data or procedures and a lack of business reputation.

Diagnosis:

From the process of risk control, we do two unique analyses that comprise:

- Threat Evaluation
- Risk Evaluation
    - Quantitative Analysis
    - Qualitative Analysis

Threat Evaluation:

Threat evaluation is a process of analyzing the resources of cyber threats and evaluating them in relation to the data system's vulnerabilities. The aim of this analysis is to recognize the threats that threaten a specific data system in a particular environment.

It consists of four measures that include:

- Define the real threat.
- Identify potential consequences to the business if the danger is accomplished.
- Ascertain the likely frequency of a hazard.
- Evaluate the likelihood that a hazard will really materialize.

A company must be well prepared for all kind of dangers, the amount and kinds of dangers can be overpowering but may typically be categorized as

Organic: Earthquakes, floods, hurricanes, lightning, fire, etc.

Man-made: Unauthorized access, data entry mistakes, strikes/labour disputes, terrorism, theft, social technology, malicious code and viruses, and so forth.

Risk Evaluation:

The following element in risk management is risk evaluation. A threat analysis brings together with the components of hazard management (identification, evaluation, and management) and is essential to a company for developing a successful risk management plan.

It consists of four measures that include:

Describe the resources to be protected, such as their comparative price, endurance, or value to your organization. This is a part of risk identification (asset evaluation).

Define certain threats, including hazard frequency and impact information. This is a part of risk identification (hazard investigation).

Calculate Annualized Loss Expectancy (ALE).

Select proper safeguards. This is a part of both hazard identification and Risk Management.

The Annualized Loss Expectancy (ALE) provides a standard, Quantifiable measure of the effect a realized hazard has on a company's assets. ALE is very helpful for ascertaining the cost-benefit ratio of control or guard. ALE is determined by this formula:

Single Loss Expectancy (SLE) x Annualized Rate of Occurrence (ARO) = Annualized Loss Expectancy (ALE)

Where:

Single Loss Expectancy (SLE) is a measure of the loss incurred by one recognized threat or occasion, expressed in dollars. It's calculated as Asset Value ($) x Exposure Factor (EF).

Exposure Factor (EF) is a measure of this adverse effect or effect a recognized threat or event could have on a particular advantage, expressed as a proportion.

Annualized Rate of Occurrence (ARO) is your estimated yearly frequency of occurrence for a hazard or occasion.

Aims of Risk Evaluation:

The procedure for conducting a hazard analysis is quite much like identifying an acceptable risk level. Basically, you do a hazard analysis about the business as a whole to ascertain the acceptable risk level.

A threat analysis has four Chief aims:

- Identify assets and their worth.
- Identify vulnerabilities and risks.
- Measure the likelihood and business effect of the possible dangers.
- Supply an economic balance between the impact of the threat and the Expense of this countermeasure.

Identify assets and their values:

From the process of identifying assets and its own worth, we believe that the value Put on resources (like data), what function was asked to build it, how much it costs to preserve, what harm would result if it had been lost or ruined, and what advantage another party would gain if it were to get it.

Knowing the value of an asset is the first step to knowing what security mechanisms must be set in place and what funds must go toward protecting it.

These issues must be considered when assigning values to resources:

- Price to obtain or develop the advantage
- Price to Keep and protect the strength
- Worth of the advantage to users and owners
- Worth of the advantage to adversaries

- Worth of intellectual property which went into creating the data
- Cost others are willing to pay for the advantage
- Price to replace the advantage if misplaced
- Operational and manufacturing activities which are influenced if the advantage is inaccessible
- Liability problems if the advantage is compromised
- Usefulness and function of this advantage in the company

Identify vulnerabilities and risks:

After the resources have been identified and assigned values, All those vulnerabilities and related threats will need to be identified that may influence each asset's integrity, confidentiality or accessibility requirements.

There's a lot of vulnerabilities and risks that may impact the various resources, it's essential in order to correctly categorize and prioritize them to ensure the many crucial items can be cared for first.

Quantify the likelihood and business effect of those potential dangers:

The staff carrying out the risk assessment needs to determine the organization's effect of the identified risks. To estimate possible losses posed by dangers, answer these questions:

What bodily harm could the danger trigger, and also how much could that cost?

How much expansion reduction could the hazard cause, and also how much could that Price?

- What's the value lost if private information is revealed?
- What's the price of recovering from a virus attack?
- What's the price of recovering from a hacker attack?
- What's the value lost if necessary apparatus were to neglect?
- What's your single loss expectancy (SLE) for each asset and every threat?

These are a few general queries, while the particular questions will depend Upon the kinds of dangers that the team finds. The group then must figure out the likelihood and frequency of the identified vulnerabilities being exploited.

Identify countermeasures and decide cost/benefit:

The group then must identify countermeasures and alternatives to Decrease the Possible damages against the recognized threats. A safety countermeasure must make decent business sense, meaning it is cost-effective and its advantage outweighs its price. This requires another kind of investigation: a cost/benefit investigation.

A Widely Used cost/benefit calculation could be provided:

Worth of safeguard into the company =

(ALE before implementing shield) -- (ALE after applying protector) -- (the yearly price of the shield)

For Instance, if the ALE of this danger of a hacker bringing a webserver Is $12,000 before implementing the proposed safeguard, $3,000 following implementing the protector, and the yearly expense of upkeep and operation of this protector is $650, and then the worth of the safeguard to the provider is $8,350 annually.

These items have to be considered and assessed when deriving the complete price of a countermeasure:

- Merchandise costs
- Design/planning prices
- Implementation prices
- Environment modifications
- Compatibility with different countermeasures
- Care requirements
- Testing demands
- Repair, replacement or upgrade prices
- Running and service costs
- consequences on productivity

It's important that the staff knows how to calculate the real cost of a countermeasure to correctly weigh it against the advantage and savings that the countermeasure is assumed to supply.

The following is a brief list of what is anticipated from the results of a hazard analysis:

- Monetary values assigned to resources
- A comprehensive collection of possible and important dangers
- Probability of the incidence rate of every threat
- reduction potential the corporation may endure per threat at a 12-month period span
- Recommended protects, countermeasures, and action

Risk evaluation can be divided into two big forms:

- Quantitative Risk Evaluation
- Enforcement Risk Evaluation

Quantitative Risk Evaluation:

A Quantitative risk analysis tries to assign a goal numeric price (price) to the elements (assets and dangers) of this hazard analysis. In quantitative hazard analysis all facets of this procedure, including strength value, affect, hazard frequency, protect effectiveness, protect costs, uncertainty, and odds are quantified and assigned a numerical value. But, achieving a strictly qualitative risk analysis is hopeless.
Qualitative Risk Analysis:

A qualitative risk analysis is scenario-driven and does not try to assign numerical values to the elements (assets and dangers) of this hazard analysis. In qualitative hazard analysis, we create actual situations that explain a threat and possible losses to organizational resources. Unlike a quantitative hazard analysis, it is possible to run a strictly qualitative hazard analysis.
Control:

So far as CISSP is worried, the candidate should know all of the core components of risk management which also has control. Risk Control is a shield or countermeasure that reduces risk related to a particular threat. Not having a shield against a hazard creates vulnerability and raises the risk.

Risk management could be achieved through a number of three overall treatments.

Risk reduction:

Mitigating risk by implementing the essential security controls, policies, and approaches to protect an advantage. This may be accomplished by changing, reducing, or removing the danger and/or vulnerability linked to the risk.

Risk mission:

To prevent the results of danger, we could assign the potential loss related using a danger to another party, like an insurance provider.

Risk endorsement:

It includes the approval of this reduction related to a possible risk.

Nonetheless, in risk management, we mitigate the dangers that itself shouldn't introduce new vulnerabilities. It is a continuous process that has to be run by organizations to be able to prevent cyber attacks. The aforementioned management methods and procedures are fundamental and basic and can also be contained in the CISSP examination by International Information Systems Security Certification Consortium.

Application Security risk assessment and risk management are critical activities for IT managers. Corporations face increased levels of Software Safety threat from hackers and cyber crooks looking for intellectual property and customer details. An extensive program security hazard assessment is a modern-day business requirement.

Application Security risk management provides the best protection within the limitations of funding law, ethics, and security. Performing a general Application Security threat assessment allows organizations to make sensible choices.

Internet Programs - Program Safety

Internet Servers are among the most crucial resources of Application Security threats to organizations. Performing a program security evaluation and applying safety risk management is crucial. Listed below are core factors that pose a Significant security risk to Program Security.

Default Setup - Program Safety

Internet Server default settings which might not be protected render unneeded databases, templates, administrative instruments, etc. open to attacks. Inadequate program security risk management renders safety breaches for hackers to take full control over the Web server.

Databases - Program Security

Internet sites and software have to be interactive to be helpful and there is the threat... Web software without adequate software security permit hackers to attack their databases. Invalid input scripts contribute to many of those worst database strikes. Extensive risk assessment may disclose action to guarantee program security.

Encryption - Program Security

Encryption Reduces application safety dangers and declines when Internet servers are broken. Although an organization's Intranet server has higher exposure to attacks, encryption makes a lower relative risk.

The increase of the IT sector has given rise to work for several engineers specialized in a variety of fields tagged as a requirement by the companies to elevate the business to a different level entirely. This enhancement of the sector alongside gives rise to different potential risks that may easily attack the functioning system of the provider.

IT Business is a growing industry using IT professionals for a variety of requirements in the business. How well-educated professionals will be necessary for a business for driving in earnings by using their wisdom and data storage is a must in a software company to safeguard their information similarly security and threat management is vital to maintain the working environment healthily and lucrative.

It's very simple for any software company to receive drawn to several computer-related dangers so that they need to be well-armed with all the available instruments and goods in the marketplace to safeguard them from being assaulted and correctly deal with the security risks related to their information technology resources. Numerous dangers can appear like: Because of fire the workplace is left with burnt documents and networked computers or a document is circulated stating the server is down due to the water rushing from the ceiling or machines containing sensitive information are hijacked through the system. The aim of the list down the dangers that could pop up would be always to question this, how ready is your company to mitigate these dangers and react appropriately, even if any of those events happen? Given the critical safety risks to information technology resources, handling these risks efficiently is a vital job for the company and its various sections. The procedure will benefit, the individual departments and the whole company as a whole. It's necessary that management needs to understand what dangers exist within their own IT environment, and how those risks can be lowered or removed.

When it comes to repairing technical problems with the assistance of numerous IT goods and handles the safety and manages the dangers that may prove harmful to the business, especially computers, safety and risk management specialist is the individual to contact. Security & Risk Management teams provide alternatives that address business demand challenges and work on crucial areas like regulatory and compliance program direction, identity & access management.

Safety & risk management groups tackle issues associated with safety risk assessment, safety health check, safety workshop, and data security framework actions. The professionals coping with them need to be well equipped with all the several tools offered on the market to assist them in this process that would help the business in healthily functioning.

Together with the growing business, computers being infected by dangers are a clear circumstance except to keep the safety and deal with the threat is the trick to the profitable firm. Nevertheless, the requirement for these specialists is actually large and so, a lot of curious individuals can be part of the experience.

Domain 1 -- Security and Risk Management

References to ISO standards and NIST files start within this domain name and continue across the remaining domain names. You have to compile a listing of lists to your research manual. I place them here, together with lists of regulations.

As I always tell people: to be aware, you ought to be aware that the Torah is your scripture of Judaism, the Quran is the scripture of Islam, the Vedas would be the scripture of Hinduism, and so forth. You do not need to really read some of them to understand that. Nor should you browse one of these documents. Just have the ability to match their titles or amounts to what they are about.

Yellow means quite likely to look on the test, gravy means less probable, not coloured means moderate chances, all these being my very best guess, what I'd use if I needed to re-take the examination.

- ISO Standards

- ISO 15026

- Systems and Software Engineering

- ISO 15288

- Systems and Software Engineering

- ISO 17889

- Defines Cloud computing, such as NIST and Naas or even Network-as-a-Service.

- ISO 27000

- Perhaps not Mentioned much, appears to be less or more a dictionary.

- ISO 27001

- Details Security Management System, defines exactly what "protected" means.

- ISO 27002

- Guidance And best methods to earn ISO 27001 occur.

- ISO 27005

- Information Security Risk Management.

- ISO 31000

- Risk Direction -- Principles and Techniques.

- NIST Records

- SP 800-37

- Risk Management Framework

- SP 800-53

- Catalogue of privacy and security controls (safety toolkit)

- SP 800-60

- Guide to Mapping Kinds of Information and Data Systems to Security Categories

- SP 800-63
- The Way to do identity proofing and registration
- SP 800-88
- Strategies for Media Sanitization
- SP 800-160
- System Security Engineering
- FIPS
- U.S. Government Federal Information Processing Standards.
- FIPS 140-2

Certifies cryptographic hardware and software. Four levels Of increasing safety:

- ✓ FIPS 140-2 Level 1 = proper implementation
- ✓ FIPS 140-2 Level 2 = tamper-evident
- ✓ FIPS 140-2 Level 3 = tamper-resistant
- ✓ FIPS 140-2 Level 4 = automated zeroizing, ardently tamper-resistant even at a complex lab surroundings

FIPS 199

Categorizes U.S. national data based on the Effect Of violations of its confidentiality, integrity, and accessibility.

FIPS 200

Minimum Security Requirements for Federal Information and Information Systems
SCAP, OVAL, and STIGs

U.S. NIST established SCAP, a protocol and criteria and nomenclature for analyzing and reporting on software vulnerabilities and configuration issues.

XCCDF and OVAL are reporting languages and formats.

CPE, CCE, CVE (and many others) are enumerations characterized by MITRE on behalf of the U.S. Government. CVSS and CCSS are connected with conservation scoring systems.

NVD or National Vulnerability Database is managed by NIST.
Additional Standards and Records and Groups

COBIT

The best way to handle and record Enterprise IT and IT security work.

COSO

Founded in reaction to striking and acute financial sector scandals From the U.S. from the 1980s, to tackle financial reporting fraud and disputes.

CSA STAR

A company's listing of cloud Support Suppliers with tiers:

"We are safe since we did a questionnaire so expect us"

Assessed by an external auditor accredited by CSA.

Continuously tracked, possibly about to eventually arrive in late 2019.

ENISA

The network of community and data security experience for your E.U., Its member nations, and its own private sector and taxpayers.

ICASA

Publishes IT RISK frame, joins strategic business standpoint with IT Administration.

ITIL

An agency delivery collection of Best practices, cantered on company objectives.

ITU

Inner Telecommunication Union -- standardizes communication technologies.

Uptime Institute

Accreditation for data centres, the information in their layout.

Regulations

The (ISC)2 CCSP certificate enter further details about those. This includes how the E.U. GDPR is very strict. And many nations already had, or shortly enacted, privacy legislation at least as stringent as GDPR, therefore E.U. information can easily be exported to them for processing: Australia, New Zealand, Argentina, Japan, Switzerland, and also a few others.

APEC (or Asia-Pacific Economic Cooperation) in East Asian nations desiring To be safe enough to do business without getting in the way of their company itself. If you have seen Hong Kong company, from neon-lit glass towers into the night markets, then this isn't hard to remember.

The OECD helps governments and governments around the world cope with Improving social and economic well-being, in addition, it balances privacy with gain.

Meanwhile, the U.S. has been completely no warranty of Solitude. Safe Harbour got no regard, its replacement Privacy Shield was not much better. U.S. companies have the ability to do global business with particular contract clauses asserting E.U.-level protection.

FedRAMP

U.S. national requirement attached to FISMA, regulating the purchase and usage of other and cloud-managed IT services.

FISMA

U.S. national law applying only to Government agencies, requiring them to comply with NIST standards.

GDPR

E.U. stringent requirements for solitude, as international law.

GLBA

U.S. national law requiring banks to safeguard customer information.

HIPAA

U.S. national law about medical personal information.

PIPEDA

Canadian national requirement to safeguard privacy.

Sarbanes-Oxley a.k.a. Sarbox, SOX

U.S. federal requirements made in reaction to dramatic Financial frauds in the 1990s.
Legal Counsel

Due Maintenance vs Due Diligence
- ✓ Due Diligence -- Investigating and preparation, done beforehand.
- ✓ Due Maintenance -- Conduct a reasonable and prudent person with appropriate training will work out, careful continuing operations.

Functions

A bicycle provides a helpful setting for cases:

Data Subject - the Individual to whom sensitive information refers.

Data Owner / Data Controller - the thing that collects or generates sensitive info, legally liable for the own protection. CEO or the board of directors of the hospital. The exact folks, you consider these as Controller when they're planning what information to collect and why, and as Owner when contemplating legal responsibility.

Data Steward - accountable for information content, context, and related business rules. Head of health care documents, chooses data and metadata, formats, processes for data entry. Nurses and radiology technicians follow that Steward's processes.

Data Custodian -- oversees the information daily on behalf of the owner / control. System administrators, database administrators, backup operators, and other IT staff in the hospital.

Data Processor -- passes or manipulates or transforms or Otherwise procedures sensitive information, on behalf of their owner / control. Contractor transcribing physician notes, submitting medical insurance claims, etc.

Due Diligence / Due Care

Because Diligence is planning and investigation completed originally.

Due Maintenance is an ongoing procedure maintaining exactly what a well-informed, proficient, sensible person would do to help their client.

Quantitative Risk Analysis

This is basic school analysis and mathematics, dressed up with fancy phrases and acronyms.

You've got an advantage that earns $100,000 each year. An internet site selling something, let us say.

A Specific attack could eliminate 10 percent of that.

Given previous experiences and present defences, you estimate that the assault will likely occur once every four years, normally.

So, to quantitatively examine that danger:

AV or the Asset Value is $100,000.

EF or the Length Factor is 10 percent or 0.1.

The SLE or Single Loss Expectancy is how much one effective attack expenses. Its whole value times the percentage dropped, duh. SLE = AV × EF SLE = 100,000 × 0.1 SLE = 10,000

The ARO Or Annual Cost of occurrence is how many times it is predicted to take place in a regular year. After every four years signifies 0.25 each year.

The ALE Or Annual Loss Expectancy is, duh, just how many times it is predicted to take place in a year times just how much every event expenses. ALE = SLE × ARO ALE = 10,000 × 0.25 ALE = 2,500

Then, ensure defences don't cost more than this annually. Do not invest a dollar to spare a nickel.

STRIDE

It is a contrived acronym: Spoofing individuality, Tampering with information, Repudiation, Info disclosure, Denial of support, Elevation of privilege

Octave

By CMU, for seeing overall risk across a company -- not as likely to look on evaluation.

DLP vs DRM

DRM protects intellectual property. You cannot see this DVD. Despite the fact that you've seen it dozens of times and contributed to the Wikipedia article describing it.

DLP protects keys. This record cannot depart headquarters. It is the script for another movie in the show, which will be going to filming.

Instruction, Training, Awareness

- ✓ Instruction

Formal Courses, usually in an accredited academic institution.

- ✓ Coaching

1-to-5 Day classes presented by subject matter specialists, typically working for for-profit training suppliers.

- ✓ Awareness

Informal, Brief, to remind and promote workers.

CHAPTER TWO
ASSETS SECURITY

Asset security falls to the next domain of CISSP examination and constitutes 12.5percent of those questions for this exam. Asset security comprises the concepts, structures, principles, and criteria directed at tracking and procuring assets, and people Controls that apply several levels of confidentiality, accessibility, and integrity.

By definition, an advantage is anything that could be significant to the business, like spouses, employees, equipment, facilities, and data. Info is usually the main asset to any business or business and is Valuable to each information system. Information moves through the organization's data system and has to be disposed of appropriately after it's no more of use.

But, CISSP Applicants must know the core theories of asset security and their software. These topics are contained in this domain name:

- ✓ Data Management: Keep and ascertain possession.
- ✓ Longevity and use: Data Security, access, sharing, and publishing.
- ✓ Data Standards: Data lifecycle management, specification, storage, and arching.
- ✓ Make sure Proper Retention: Media, employees, and hardware, business data retention policies.
- ✓ Determine Data Security Controls: Info in the rest, the information in transit, tailoring and scoping.

Information Classification

The crucial metadata Items which are connected to associations' valuable info are a classification level. The classification label stays affixed through the info life-cycle (Acquisition, Use, Archival, and Disposal) and guarantees that the security of data.

The phrases used to categorize data are "criticality,""sensitivity," sometimes in conjunction. The "sensitivity" of data is compromised if unauthorized people access it. By way of instance, the data losses endured by the associations, like the Office of Personnel Management and the National Security Agency. On the flip side, critical advice is vital for the operation of any company. As an example, a firm, Code Spaces, which provided code services in 2014, was closed down when unauthorized people deleted their code repositories.

Exam Suggestion: The destruction and managing requirements are different for each classification level.

The organization can Pick the classification amount, Nonetheless, it is dependent upon if it's a commercial company or military service. The common heights of a commercial company and military information demand:

    Public info could be looked at by the public and, hence, the disclosure of the data couldn't result in any harm. By way of instance, the general public may know about the business's upcoming projects.
    Sensitive information requires extraordinary precautions to guarantee confidentiality and ethics for its own protection. By way of instance, sensitive

information could incorporate the company's financial details.

Personal information could consist of personal data, including credit card information and bank account. Unauthorized disclosure could be catastrophic.

Confidential data is only used inside the business and, even in the instance of unauthorized disclosure, the company could endure significant consequences.

Unclassified data Isn't sensitive, like recruitment information in the army.

Secret advice, if revealed, can adversely impact national security, like the launch of army deployment programs.

Best covert data, if revealed, could cause huge harm to national security, like the disclosure of spy satellite details.

Exam Suggestion: The terms "sensitive" and "personal" Are typically connected with non-governmental organizations (NGOs) as well as the phrases "top secret", "key," and "unclassified" are associated with government agencies.

Caution: The classification principle has to be applied to information no matter its structure; it isn't important if the information is sound, video, fax, electronic, paper, etc..

Data Ownership

The transit of data must finish Its life cycle. The many entities which produce the life cycle effective comprise the data owners, data custodian, system operator, security secretary, manager, and consumer. Each has a special function in protecting the business's assets.

The Data Owner, or Info Owner, is a supervisor who ensures data security and decides that the classification level. In addition, he decides whether the information remains in hard-copy or soft-copy form.

The System Owner controls the functioning of the computer that stores information. This requires hardware and software configurations, like handling system upgrades, patches, etc.

The Data Custodian performs regular data backups and Recovery and preserves safety, like the configuration of anti-virus programs.

The Safety Administrator assigns consent and Manages information on a community.

Users have to comply with principles, compulsory policies, criteria, and procedures. As an example, the user shouldn't discuss his accounts or other private information with other co-workers.

The Manager, or User Supervisor, is accountable for Assessing the actions of all of the entities above.

Retention Policies

Data security requires That sensitive information, when processed for any purpose, shouldn't be maintained for a longer period. Regrettably, there's absolutely no universal agreement on how long the company ought to retain data. On the other hand, the legal and regulatory requirements change among business communities and states. Every company needs to follow information retention policies to thwart disaster, especially when dealing with the impending or ongoing litigations.

Cases of retention policies include:

- The State of Florida Electronic Records and Records Management Practices, 2010
- The European Records Retention Guide, 2012

How to Create a Retention Policy?

There are three basic questions that every retention coverage needs to reply:

How to conserve info: The information must be held in a fashion so that it's accessible whenever demanded. To create this accessibility sure, the company should think about some issues, such as:

The Taxonomy is your strategy for information classification. This classification entails various classes, for instance, operational (human resource, product improvements), the organizational (executive, marriage employee), or any mixture of them.

The normalization develops tagging strategies that guarantee that the information is searchable. In reality, non-normalized information is stored in a variety of formats like sound, video, PDF documents, etc.

How Long to Maintain Info: The classical information retention strength approaches were: "the keep that which" circle and "the store nothing" camp. But in contemporary times, these strategies are still curable in many conditions, especially when an organization experiences litigation.

What information to maintain: The information associated with company management, third party deals, or venture is beneficial for any company. In addition, the counsellor opinion has overriding importance, because he indicates that what information is helpful in case of litigation.

Protecting Privacy

Following the injury of the 9/11 strikes in Nyc, many nations moved towards Safety rather than solitude. On the other hand, the safety flows of Edward Snowden, in 2013, closely encouraged the states to concentrate on toward greater privacy protection. Several organizations believe both privacy and security in their data systems.

Data Owners play a crucial part of privacy protection as they directly or indirectly decide that has access to specific data.

Data remnants are still abandoned after the deletion of information and they can badly sabotage privacy. In reality, the information deletion operation only marks the memory available for different data without erasing the initial data. There are four strategies used to cancel info remanence:

Overwriting creates the initial data unrecoverable by substituting its memory place (the pattern of 0's and 1's) using the random or fixed patterns of 0's and 1's.

Degaussing eliminates the magnetic field patterns on disc drives with magnetic force. Because of this, the initial information is wiped and unrecoverable.

Encryption gets the data unusable even after deletion since the secret is always connected to information that's only available to the proprietor of information.

Physical devastation is accomplished if the physical networking is ruined using the shredding technique.

Limits on collection: Associations must accumulate at a minimum amount of information, as it could be an issue of law in the future. In 2014, over a hundred nations passed privacy security laws that influence organizations within their own jurisdictions. The coverages differ among nations; for instance, Argentina has the most restrictive solitude, while China has no limitations in any way.

Data Security Controls

Deciding data security controllers is a Herculean job. But, the criteria, scoping, and therefore are used to pick the controls. Additionally, restraint's conclusion is influenced by the circumstance either the information remains in motion, at rest, or in usage.

Scoping and Tailoring: Scoping is a process to find out that standard will be employed by the company. The tailoring assists in assessing the standard for associations.

Data in movement is information that has been transmitted across the network, while information at rest is saved on the hard disk. Either kind requires unique controls for security.

Drive Encryption is the controller for the security of Information in the rest. This controller is suggested for the majority of media and mobile devices which include confidential information.

Media transportation and storage supplies information security through backup and eases data storage offsite through physical motion or through networks.

Managing Requirements

Managing requirements include appropriate marking, managing, Storing, and destroying sensitive websites beneath the policies and processes.
Data Security

The most precious asset of a company is its own information when collateral professionals start considering data safety; they generally begin considering the safety controls used to protect the confidentiality, integrity, and accessibility of resources holding the information of a company.

Securing data at rest: Statistics at rest is information stored somewhere for later usage. Even though the data sets aren't being used at the present time, Safety professionals have to have the ability to protect against most of the schemes the attacker attempts to steal information.

Data in movement is information that's used and can be traversing across a community medium. Data in motion has to be protected against eavesdropping attacks.

Matters to do to protect your company's information

Have clear policies and processes surrounding the proper use of information.
Different Kinds of encryption for different surroundings to safeguard sensitive data
Access controls to limit access to info

Data safety policy crucial standards

Policies must offer the foundational authority for information security attempts adding validity to your own work and supplying hammer if necessary to guarantee compliance.

Policies provide advice on the right avenues to follow when requesting access to information for business purposes.

Policies also need to possess an exception procedure for officially requesting policy exceptions if required to fulfil business requirements.

Crucial issues data protection coverage should cover

Data classification coverages: Describes the safety levels of data employed in a company and the procedure for assigning data to a certain classification level. These classes are assigned according to the sensitivity of this data and the criticality of the information to your enterprise.

Data storage policies: Data storage is an integral part of safety coverage. It describes to the consumers the proper storage areas for information of varying classification levels. By way of instance, the policy may restrict the usage of cloud storage alternatives for sensitive information.

Data storage policies ought to additionally address access management requirements for stored data, including the procedure used to get access to data as well as the mechanisms used to apply access controls.

Data Transmission policies shield data in movement; it must cover what information might be transmitted over various sorts of programs and under what jurisdiction.

Data lifecycle policies provide significant advice about the end of life process such as advice. This is significant since data may keep sensitivity after the company no longer needs it. Data lifecycle policies must contain information retention policies, data disposal policies.

Data safety functions -- Many Distinct individuals throughout the Organization play a part in protecting data.

Data Owner- Can Be a senior-level official/business pioneer that has overall responsibility for its corresponding datasets. They generally assign that responsibility to some data steward for nitty-gritty decisions of information governance.

Data Steward- Data steward, manages the execution of the high tech policies determined by the information owner. They may make day to day choices about who may get into a dataset. Typically, there's a reporting connection between the information owner as well as the information steward.

Data Custodian-Would be the people who really store and process the data in question they're also called data chips. Technologists tend to be data custodians for virtually all of the information in the business on account of the nature of their tasks.

Data Privacy -There are ten principles summarized by generally accepted Privacy Principles (GAPP)

Control - Organization managing private data should have proper policies, processes, and governance arrangements in place to guard the privacy of their data

Notice - The company offers notice to the Information issues regarding its privacy policies and processes and indicates the functions for which data has been collected and utilized.

Option and Consent - The thing should notify data subjects of the choice about the information that they have and receive approval (implicit or explicit) from these folks for the collection, storage, use, and sharing of the information.

The group - The selection of personal information functions must disclose in their privacy notices from the organization.

Utilization, Retention, and Disposal- The company should keep personal information provided that it's required then information must be disposed of safely

Accessibility - Organizations should provide patient access to their own data with the capacity to examine and upgrade whenever desire.

Disclosure to Third Parties - The data is shared with third parties from the company if this sharing is consistent with intentions revealed in privacy notices plus they have the explicit or tacit permission of the person to share that info.

Safety - It is the organization's duty to procure private data against unauthorized access, either logically or physically.

Quality - Your company should take suitable actions to guarantee the personal information that they keep is accurate, complete, and applicable.

Tracking and Enforcement - The company needs to have a schedule set up to track compliance with its privacy policies and supply procedures to tackle disputes pertaining precisely to the same.

Data Security Controls

Safety baselines - supply enterprises with a powerful method to define the safety criteria for calculating systems and economically apply those criteria across the installed apparatus. It needs to be

    Generic - All these generic baselines are extremely useful during many instances when fresh media devices are introduced to an IT Infrastructure for the very first moment.
    Complete - These will be the safety baselines for your operating systems, cellular technologies, network appliances, devices, and other programs that are generally utilized in their own surroundings.

Tracking - 24 x 7 X 365 tracking is required after the baselines are established. Different factors like users inadvertently adjust settings; attackers undermine safety, etc. could cause deviations from this baseline.

Taking advantage of Accessible Business Standards - Safety Configuration criteria may contain n number of configurations that specialists advocate improving system safety, and its time consuming to make the documentation to the exact same. Organizations can save hundreds of hours of effort by obeying the available criteria from these resources:

    Vendor - individuals who make devices, programs, they know their products better than anybody else, plus they have a vested interest in assisting you and your company firmly. For instance - Microsoft Security Compliance Manager.
    Government Agencies - Government also spends quite a lot of time and energy developing safety standards such as NIST.
    Independent Organizations - Some entities need a much more objective source compared to the authorities and seller and search out third party

organizations which exist solely to give security guidance, by way of instance, CIS.

Customizing Security Standards - Customization on the present criteria will depend upon the organization's possess safety and business needs, but the notion is they don't have to compose a whole standard from scratch. They could simply reference a current standard and after that only note the gaps where controllers are added, altered or eliminated.

File Permissions - This is a form of access control that allows the easy Authorities of the organization's security policies by restricting data access on an as-needed basis.

Windows file system
- Complete Control: Read, Write and Execute permissions are allowed.
- Read: Documents can only be read rather than altered.
- Read & Execute: The end-user can't just browse the document, but can start it also.
- Compose: Documents can be modified and written.
- Modify: is a mixture Read & Execute and Write permissions and has the capability to delete.

Linux file system
- Chow alters a directory or file user proprietor.
- Chirp alters a directory or file group owner.
- Chemed alters the permissions on a directory or file

Linux utilizes three distinct permissions for every file the Read consent -- r, Compose consent -w, and Execute permission-x, then utilizes letter abbreviations for every form of proprietor the user operator, abbreviated with a un, the Group Owner, abbreviated with a gram and the rest of the users, abbreviated having an o.

Encryption - In easy words encryption could be described as the conversion of plain text to cipher text with a mathematical algorithm. Encryption Ought to Be implemented to the next

- Total disk encryption
- Database encryption
- Hardware encryption

Note: Cloud info protection - Organizations must stick to the exact same safety controls to the information stored at the cloud since it would data saved in their own data centre.

Information Classification - Information classification policies explain the safety levels of data employed in a company and the procedure for assigning data to a certain classification level. The various security classes or classifications utilized by an organization determine the proper storage handling and accessibility requirements for classified data.

Army or government Sector Classification of Information

- o Best Secret
- o Secret
- o Confidential
- o Sensitive but Unclassified or SBU
- o Unclassified

Private or commercial Sector Classification of Information

- Confidential
- Personal
- Sensitive
- Public

An asset Is something that has some value to an organization. It has individuals, partners, equipment, facilities, standing, and data. A via details on asset was mentioned in Domain Name 1: Security & Risk Management additionally within our previous site. Refer to ythe cited hyperlink for additional information. As mentioned in prior sites in the context of Risk Management While each advantage has to be shielded, this site focuses on protecting data resources. Info /Information is generally the most precious asset and is located in the middle of each data system, therefore precision concentrate on its own security makes much sense.

- Data Life-cycle
- Establish Sensitive Information
- The requirement for classification and its own procedure
- Identify Data function
- Data Security Policy
- Knowing different Data conditions and their Security mechanism
- Labelling Sensitive Info
- Storing Sensitive Information
- Destroying Sensitive Info
- Data Retention
- Data Protection with Encryption
- Selecting Security controls -- Typical
- Selecting Security controls -- Baseline

- Selecting Security controls -- Configuration/Change/Patch Management

Let Us know - What's "Information" - Quite simply; we could declare "A Data that's combined to form a few significances." Once information is generated; It moves through the whole life-cycle within an Organization. Hence, we'll start with Info life-cycle. Data goes through numerous stages. Hence, the CIA ought to be guaranteed at each step.

To Address the CIA efficiently and efficiently, we must know sensitive Info for the sake of the Organization.

Thus, the Initial step in Asset Security would be to Classify and revaluate the advantage.

Refer to undermind map for Information Life-cycle, Sensitive Data, Data Classification, and Its Procedure.

CHAPTER THREE
SECURITY ARCHITECTURE AND ENGINEERING

Security Architecture and Engineering is an Essential element of Domain Name # 3 at the CISSP examination. It counts for a great chunk of this, as 13 percent of the subjects within this domain name are covered on the examination. However, aside from that, the understanding gained from this specific domain gives a crucial, basic background for virtually any kind or type of cybersecurity professionals.

Listed below is a list of knowledge areas the aspiring CISSP-certified Individual needs to have at least a baseline understanding of.

Security Engineering

As the CISSP examination questions can also be scenario-based, you must be able to understand the fundamentals and employ them Secure Design Basics Incorporating safety into the design procedure

Security engineers try to retrofit a current system with safety features designed to safeguard the confidentiality, integrity, and availability of the information managed by that program.

Subject/object version

In this approach, each access request is viewed as having two separate Elements: a subject who's asking some form of accessibility and an item that's the source being requested.

Failure modes

There are two potential failure modes:

1. Fail open platform. In the event the safety controls fail, they're automatically bypassed
2. Fail a protected system. This is where a safety controller fails, and the machine down itself to a country where no access is allowed

Security Designs

This region of the domain could be considered theoretical in character. Nevertheless, It's still true that you should get an understanding of these, as the CISSP examination will cover them to a level or another. It's necessary to be aware that this not a comprehensive collection of the safety versions; you need to consult with your research publication or boot camp notes to receive all the specifics of each one the applicable models.

- Bell-Lavandula security version
- Biba integrity model
- Lattice-Based Access controls
- design versions
- Clark-Wilson
- Information Flow model
- Chinese Wall version
- Non-interference version
- Take-Grant Protection version
- The Access Control Matrix
- Zachman Framework for Enterprise Architecture
- Graham-Denning version
- Harrison-Ruzz-Ullman version

Safety Requirements

In addition, you need to comprehend the following, about the approval procedure in a company concerning how a certain could be deployed and executed:

    Certification. Here is the practice of discovering a tech product fulfils the needs of a specific amount of certificate. It's a government-wide choice that a product meets specific security conditions
    Accreditation. That is a choice made after accreditation, and It's a particular choice regarding whether a tech system may be Utilized in a Particular environment

Cloud Computing and Virtualization

As you prepare for the CISSP examination, you also need to comprehend that the significance of the 3 households of cloud computing systems, that can be as follows:

- Personal cloud
- Public cloud
- Hybrid

Organizations adopting a hybrid approach use a combination of people along with a personal cloud. Within this version, they can use the people to get a few computing workloads, but they also run their own personal cloud for different workloads.

High Availability and Fault Tolerance

For any security practitioner, the fundamentals of having systems that are redundant and Mitigating failures is of prime importance, and can be assessed as follows:

The core notion of high accessibility is using operationally redundant systems occasionally at several places, such as using a bunch of net functions in place that may continue to function even if one server fails

Fault tolerance, on the other hand, helps protects one system from failing at the first place by making it resilient at the terms of technical failures

Server and Client Vulnerabilities

Most companies and corporations have some Kind of client-server network topology. That is where lots of workstations and wireless apparatus (the customers) are attached to a central server to ensure tools could be retrieved efficiently. Given that this amount of significance in the actual world, this can be a somewhat heavily weighted part on the CISSP examination. You ought to have a firm grasp of these theories:

Customer security problems

Applets. Applets written in languages such as Java and Microsoft's ActiveX include some severe safety problems, as they allow a remote site run code on your own PC. Because of this, most safety professionals advocate against using applets

Neighbourhood caching. A cache is a local shop of information that browser uses to speed up things by removing redundant lookups. Within an assault called cache poisoning, an attacker inserts bogus records from the DNS cache on a local computer that redirects unsuspecting users of the computer to bogus sites. Similar Kinds of attacks may occur for the address resolution protocol, also for documents retrieved from the online .

Server security Difficulties

Safety professionals must be Conscious of safety Problems That are specific to particular surroundings. All servers are influenced by the data flow controller, whilst database servers also have to be shielded again aggregation, inference, and other database-specific strikes.

There are two particular kinds of attacks that are specific to database servers, and are consequently important to learn for the CISSP examination:

   Aggregation. Aggregation occurs when a person with a low-level safety column can piece together details available at that reduced level to ascertain an extremely sensitive piece of advice he or she shouldn't have access to
   Inference. Inference occurs when an individual can find out sensitive information in the facts available to their

Internet Security

For cybersecurity professionals, internet security vulnerabilities are among the trickiest issues to handle. The Open Web Application Security Project (OWASP) keeps a listing of the best 10 net security vulnerabilities the CISSP exam-taker should know and ought to understand the protection mechanism for exactly the exact same. The present version of the OWASP top 10 was created in 2017.

Mobile Security

Given the significance of smartphones in our private and professional Lives, keeping them protected from cyberattacks is essential. Given light of the CISSP examination covers crucial mobile security concepts that the candidate has to know about, such as the next. Please be aware that once more, this isn't a comprehensive list, therefore it's extremely crucial that you consult with a CISSP study novel or boot camp substance to learn more.

Mobile device safety

- Mobile devices need to be shielded with one or more access control mechanisms, like passcodes and biometric fingerprint authentication
- Apparatus encryption
- Capability to eliminate the contents of your device over the system also referred to as distant wiping.
- Automated screen-lock after a certain period of inactivity
- User lockout when wrong passcode is entered too many times

Mobile device management

Mobile device management (MDM) solutions provide organizations with a simple way to handle the security settings on a lot of mobile devices concurrently. Mobile device management is a highly effective tool that enables security professionals to make sure that all apparatus used with a company's information have security settings set up that fit the company's security policy.

Mobile application security

Smartphone and tablet programs provide users a strong set of attributes that Improve their own productivity. But safety professionals have to make certain to thoroughly assess each program to make sure that its use of information meets the company's security policies. For your CISSP examination you should understand the next program safety issues:

- Mobile program authentication
- Encryption of sensitive data

Smart Device Security

Given that technology is becoming more complex and much more "smart" in nature, smart device safety is a subject covered in the CISSP examination. The candidate should have a firm grasp concerning understanding the following notions:
Industrial management systems

Industrial management systems (ICS) will be the systems and devices which control Industrial manufacturing and performance. These programs track power, gasoline, water and other utility infrastructure and manufacturing operations. Attacks on such systems may disable a country's power grid and may even ruin pieces of a town's infrastructure. For safety professionals, it is mandatory to guarantee these kinds of the industrial management systems.

- Supervisory Control and Data Acquisition (SCADA)
- Distributed Control Systems (DCS)
- Programmable Logic Controllers (PLC)

Preventing the IOT

Taking a layered approach to safety and utilizing multiple controllers to attain the very same objectives improves the chances your system will stay protected from embedded-device strikes. Following are a few safety steps for embedded devices:

- Make sure routine security upgrades (manual or automatic) for embedded devices
- Implementing safety wrappers for embedded devices
- Network segmentation for embedded devices
- Web-application firewall, as the majority of the embedded devices, have net consoles

Whatever strategy you choose, you must include control, security, Diversity and redundancy.

Cryptography

The fundamental thrust of this area of cybersecurity is assuring that data and information will soon be rendered useless if intercepted by a third party while in transit. This is where the notions of cryptography come in to play, and in truth is that an extremely optional and heavily-covered subject not just in this specific domain name, but on the CISSP examination also. Consequently, the candidate has to have a very profound comprehension of those theories. This isn't comprehensive, so once more, refer back to a CISSP study novel or boot camp training stuff.

CISSP examination takers should have an understanding of:

Symmetric cryptography

- Data Encryption Standard (DES)
- 3DES
- AES, Blowfish, and Twofish
- RC4
- Steganography

Asymmetric cryptography

- Rivest-Shamir-Adleman (RSA)
- PGP and GnuPG
- Elliptic-curve and quantum cryptography

Aims of cryptography

- Confidentiality
- Integrity
- Authentication
- Nonrepudiation

5 phases of the cryptographic life cycle

- Period I Had Initiation: Gathers the prerequisites for your new cryptographic system
- Stage II -- Development and Acquisition: Locate a Suitable mix of hardware, applications and algorithms which matches the business security goals
- Stage III -- Tests and Assessment: Configure and test the cryptographic system
- Stage IV -- Operations and Maintenance: Make sure the continued secure operation of the cryptographic system
- Stage V -- Sunset: Stage out the machine and destroy/archive keying material

Digital Rights Management

DRM utilizes encryption to leave content inaccessible to people who do not Have the essential license to see the info. It hence provides content owners with all the technical capability to avoid the unauthorized usage of the content:

Public-Key Infrastructure

Public-key infrastructure could be described as the set of functions, policies and Procedures needed to manage, produce, use, distribute, shop and revoke digital certificates and handle public-key encryption. Important features include the following:

- PKI and digital certificates
- Hash works
- Digital signatures
- How an electronic certificate is made
- How an electronic certification is revoked

Cryptanalytic Attacks

For your CISSP examination, you need to know after the cryptanalytic attacks:

- Brute-force strikes
- Knowledge-based strikes

Physical Safety

From the world of safety, we often think of it in terms of hardware, doftware, servers, database, wireless devices, smartphones etc. However, we often overlook that these things are kept in a tangible location, and such types of assumptions have to be safeguarded also. This is also a Significant Part this

CISSP examination, and the offender must have a baseline Comprehension of the following concepts:

- Website and Facility layout
- Data Center ecological controls
- Data Heart ecological security
- Physical Safety controls forms
- Physical Accessibility control
- Visitor management

CHAPTER FOUR
COMMUNICATION AND NETWORK SECURITY

INTRODUCTION

These days, government establishments, organizations and people depend progressively on PC systems, frameworks, and other associated gadgets to store, impart, and trade data. The capacity and specialized devices, generally PC or cell phone applications, are based on this trap of interconnected gadgets. This foundation establishes the multifaceted nature of security challenges on the internet. Inheritance frameworks and equipment can have exploitable infiltration that focuses on malignant aggressors. The interconnectedness of PC frameworks and applications makes it dire that cybersecurity experts learn and assess their dangers past one single measurement. Numerous data innovation experts may begin their profession in a specific authority field, for example, programming improvement, cryptography, or database the executives. As their vocation advances, the difficulties that they need to face will without a doubt grow and enhance. In this specific circumstance, the ensured data frameworks security proficient (CISSP) offers the definitive interdisciplinary preparation for the data innovation workforce. It instructs security officials to consider new ideas and procure further capabilities to upgrade the administration of cybersecurity for their organization. Correspondence and system security are one of the eight preparing areas in the CISSP accreditation.

The extent of correspondence and system innovation grows quickly. Online instalment, virtual conferencing, and remote working are a portion of the outstanding models that request steady, secure, and reliable correspondence channels. Disturbed Internet association and system spying are normal cyberattacks that can create impressive harm for the two foundations and people. The previous may lose exchange privileged insights like licensed innovation (IP) to their rivals; the last may have their bank and informal organization accounts traded off. The specialized devices and programming created on unreliable correspondence and system instruments can be troubling for the designer, yet additionally for clients. Consequently, it is imperative to comprehend the manners in which that data and information are transmitted and conveyed through PC systems. The correspondences and system security area of the CISSP cover the essentials of security worries in the system channels. Secure correspondence can be drawn nearer by means of two basic systems in PC interchanges: the protected correspondence conventions and the validation conventions. Competitors getting ready for the CISSP can move toward the subject from these two fundamental bearings.

An Overview of Secure Communication Protocols

There are several correspondence conventions that characterize rules for various machine trading data. These principles can be the sentence structure, semantics and mistake discovery of the information bundles. They guarantee the fruitful transmission of information between various substances (PCs/servers/systems). The gatherings associated with the correspondence procedure need to concur with one another so the message can go through starting with one substance then onto the next. The distinctive equipment, programming, and different gadgets utilized in this correspondence chain make it an advanced strategic arrange issues running from interoperability and multi-merchant backing to legitimate tending to. The open frameworks interconnection (OSI) model was at first created to separate the issues and dole out the obligations to seven unique layers in organize correspondence (physical, datalink, arrange, transport, session, introduction, and application). The OSI model prepared for the formation of the four-layered transmission control convention and Internet convention (TCP/IP) model (organize get to, Internet, transport, and application). The TCP/IP model is the establishment of useful and serviceable conventions for PCs and systems to communicate.

The TCP/IP model is the business standard today with more than 30 years of history. All activity frameworks bolster and work with TCP/IP conventions these days. The TCP/IP convention mix is subsequently known as "the language of the Internet." As the client populace of the Internet develops, the requirement for secure correspondence rises incredibly. Government foundations and organizations progressively embrace online correspondence frameworks to encourage exercises, for example, instalment, distinguishing proof, and application, to give some examples. Correspondence conventions between two PCs are in this way essential to protect PC systems for these computerized exercises. The accompanying conventions are a few key models created for secure correspondence on the vehicle layer of both the OSI and the TCP/IP models:

Secure Sockets Layer (SSL)

These days, PC servers and systems are required to deal with an ever-increasing number of complex online exercises. The information during the transmission pathway can chance cyberattacks, for example, wiretapping and caricaturing. In the event that the client sends delicate data, for example, a Visa number and the association between the sender and beneficiary is captured, the assailant can hold onto this data and use it. One compelling strategy to ensure this information conveyance process is encryption. SSL is a well-known encryption arrangement that gives session and lives association security between at least two gatherings. It has three goals: security assurance, personality confirmation, and unwavering quality. So as to accomplish them, SSL receives a mixture encryption technique (symmetric and deviated) to verify the correspondence between two PCs dependent on the RSA, Diffie-Hellman, or Fortezza/DMS cryptography approach. Right off the bat, the internet browser conveys a solicitation for recognizable proof to the webserver utilizing topsy-turvy encryption. The webserver answers with an affirmed position (CA) advanced authentication. In this procedure, the two sides trade a few messages to arrange the trading of keys. When the internet browser perceives the personality of the webserver by means of the CA, they will set up a symmetric encoded association with trade data. Secure HTTP or HTTPS is an application case of SSL. The location bar of the internet browser gives indications, for example, a lock symbol or green bar, to advise the clients about the security association status. A comparable convention to SSL is the basic key-administration for web convention (SKIP). The distinction among SKIP and SSL is that the previous use a built-up static mystery table to compute the keys to straightforwardly set up the ensuing secure association while the last requires earlier correspondence to create the key. The skirt was created by Sun Microsystems in 1995.

Transport Layer Security (TLS)

TLS consistently goes connected at the hip with SSL as SSL/TLS. Truth be told, TLS is the successor of SSL. The system of TLS remains significantly equivalent to SSL, however, with a few key contrasts. To begin with, TLS works on the application layer of the OSI model and the vehicle layer of the TCP/IP model. Second, the last form of SSL stops at SSL v.3.0 and the accompanying overhaul is renamed TLS v.1.0. It is imperative to manage these two issues at the top of the priority list with regards to investigate and investigate encryption issues identified with TLS. What's more, TLS embraces the keyed-hash message verification code (HMAC) encryption standard to create the key and validate messages. Fortezza encryption utilized in SSL is never again bolstered in TLS. What's more, there are more alarm messages in TLS than SSL. TLS has 23 ready portrayals while SSL has 12. Generally significant, TLS presents the TLS handshake convention, which allows the customer and server to confirm each other before trading any information.

SWIPE IP Security Protocol (SWIPE)

The convention of swipe is a test web convention security (IPsec) recommended in 1993. It is created to give start to finish information correspondence. It epitomizes every IP datagram in the correspondence with a swipe bundle convention 53 to improve the cryptography quality. The destinations of swipe were to guarantee validation, uprightness, and secrecy of IP datagrams on the system layer. It was not created to oversee keys and different approaches that happen in the correspondence procedure. Another convention with the equivalent datagram encryption reason for existing is the epitomizing security payload (ESP).

Secure Remote Procedure Call (S-RPC)

S-RPC is a protected customer server convention working on the application layer of the OSI and TCP/IP models. Numerous PC applications perform intelligently based on solicitation and reaction between the customer and server on the system. For instance, the program on the customer side demands help, the information, and different assets from the program on the server-side. At that point, the server answers the solicitation of the customer and the asynchronous connection is built up for the two gatherings. This intuitive activity is remote methodology call (RPC). The customer server activity suspends when the runtime is finished. In an
 RPC execution situation, rather than encoding the information traffic, adequately validating the customer is increasingly significant. Subsequently, the guideline of S-RPC is to create open and private keys to customers and servers for verification. The key age depends on Diffie-Hellman.

Secure Electronic Transaction (SET)

SET is a lot of conventions explicitly created to verify online monetary exchange. It basically secures charge card exchanges among buyers, dealers, and banks. The early supporters of SET were money related and internet browser specialist organizations, for example,

Mastercard, Visa, Microsoft, and Netscape. SET gives an advanced declaration as a kind of computerized wallet for each gathering to guarantee the exchange secrecy. Each declaration has a remarkable open key for their character confirmation. Every one of the information imparted by means of SET among the three gatherings is encoded so none of them can get to the touchy data. SET is profoundly well known for web-based business today. The way that Set is supported by MasterCard and Visa further increase its reducibility.

There are many conventions chipping away at different degrees of the OSI and TCP/IP organize model. SSL, TLS, SET, SKIP, swipe, and S-RPC are a portion of the key conventions that can encourage the comprehension of other correspondence conventions.

An Overview of Authentication Protocols

The component of secure correspondence conventions has a considerable accentuation on the procedure of validation. It is significant not to stir up verification with approval. The previous distinguishes the individual or association by means of username, secret word, and different gadgets. The later alludes to the entrance right of the recognized person. Validation is a definitive advance to the exclusion of everything else. Terabytes of exact and tenable data about people and money related exchanges course on the Internet consistently nowadays. Fraud and producing validation data on the internet can create a significant effect on the person in question. In this manner, validation conventions assume the job of gatekeeper in denying access to malevolent entertainers. The accompanying three models are highlight point (PPP) validation conventions:

Secret key Authentication Protocol (PAP)

PAP is an old and static secure correspondence convention utilizing plain-content passwords without encryption. It sets up the customer/server association toward the start of the correspondence. The security level of PAP is the most reduced contrasted with the other two confirmation conventions since it utilizes plain-content passwords. PAP is additionally unequipped for changing the secret word during verification once it lapses. It is utilized in circumstances and frameworks where encoded passwords are presently bolstered; for instance, some non-Windows activity frameworks and sequential line web convention (SLIP) servers. It is helpless against the most basic assaults like man-in-the-centre (MIM).

Challenge Handshake Authentication Protocol (CHAP)

CHAP is an unrivalled verification convention opposite PAP. It embraces a three-way handshake confirmation way to deal with actualize encoded validation. In addition, the confirmation is encoded by the MD5 hashing industry standard. The confirming side starts the procedure by conveying a text string to the customer side. The last at that point, produces a single direction hash an incentive on the test. The validation is recognized in like manner by the verifying side. CHAP rehashes similar validation steps routinely with alternate test esteem. Along these lines, this component can effectively ensure the confirmation procedure against playback assaults.

Extensible Authentication Protocol (EAP)

EAP can be applied past PPP to remote systems. The client demands an association through a passageway on a remote system. The character of the client is inspected and transmitted to the validation server. After accepting the data, the validation server asks the passageway to give evidence of the client's character. For whatever length of time that the passage can react to the validation server with the verification, the client will be associated with the system. EAP is a compelling customer server confirmation system. Along these lines, there are numerous adaptations of EAP, contingent upon the confirmation technique. A few instances of EAP technique are EAP-MD5, EAP-TLS and EAP-TTLS. It likewise underpins different verification systems going from token cards, smartcards, and one-time passwords to open key validation. It allows outsider merchants to make custom verification plans. Some solid models are retina examines, voice acknowledgment, and unique mark recognizable proof. The difficulties of verification require better and progressively comprehensive encryption draws near.

System security fundamentals

Definitions are fine as top-level articulations of aim. In any case, how would you spread out an arrangement for executing that vision? Stephen Northcutt composed an introduction on the rudiments of system security for CSO online over 10 years back, yet we feel unequivocal that his vision of the three periods of system security is as yet important and ought to be the hidden structure for your technique. In his telling, arrange security comprises of:

• Protection: You ought to design your frameworks and systems as effectively as could be expected under the circumstances

• Detection: You should have the option to distinguish when the setup has changed or when some system traffic demonstrates an issue

• Reaction: After recognizing issues rapidly, you should react to them and come back to a protected state as quickly as could be allowed

This, to put it plainly, is a protection top to bottom technique. In the event that there's one normal subject among security specialists, it's that depending on one single line of resistance is perilous, in light of the fact that any single guarded apparatus can be vanquished by a decided enemy. Your system isn't a line or a point: it's a domain, and regardless of whether an assailant has attacked some portion of it, despite everything you have the assets to refocus and oust them, in the event that you've sorted out your resistance appropriately.

System security techniques

To execute this sort of safeguard inside and out, there is an assortment of specific procedures and kinds of system security you will need to turn out. Cisco, a systems administration framework organization, utilizes the accompanying pattern to separate the various kinds of system security and keeping in mind that some of it is educated by their item classes, it's a helpful method to consider the various approaches to verify a system.

• Access control: You ought to have the option to square unapproved clients and gadgets from getting to your system. Clients that are allowed to organize access should just have the option to work with the restricted arrangement of assets for which they've been approved.

• Anti-malware: Viruses, worms, and trojans by definition endeavour to spread over a system, and can sneak lethargic on tainted machines for quite a long time. Your security exertion ought to give a valiant effort to anticipate beginning contamination and furthermore root out malware that makes its direction onto your system.

• Application security: Insecure applications are regularly the vectors by which aggressors gain admittance to your system. You have to utilize equipment, programming, and security procedures to secure those applications.

• Behavioural investigation: You should comprehend what typical system conduct resembles so you can spot oddities or ruptures as they occur.

• Data misfortune anticipation: Human creatures are definitely the weakest security interface. You have to execute innovations and procedures to guarantee that staff members don't intentionally or incidentally send touchy information outside the system.

• Email security: Phishing is one of the most well-known ways assailants access a system. Email security instruments can square both approaching assaults and outbound messages with touchy information.

• Firewalls: Perhaps the granddaddy of the system security world, they adhere to the guidelines you characterize to allow or deny traffic at the fringe between your system and the web, setting up an obstruction between your confided in the zone and the wild west outside. They don't block the requirement for a resistance top to the bottom system, yet they're as yet an absolute necessity have.

• Intrusion identification and anticipation: These frameworks filter organize traffic to distinguish and square assaults, frequently by connecting system action marks with databases of known assault procedures.

• Mobile gadget and remote security: Wireless gadgets have all the potential security imperfections of some other arranged device — yet additionally can associate with pretty much any remote system anyplace, requiring additional investigation.

• Network division: Software-characterized division puts arrange traffic into various groupings and makes authorizing security approaches simpler.

• Security data and occasion the executives (SIEM): These items intend to consequently pull together data from an assortment of system devices to give information you have to recognize and react to dangers.

• VPN: An instrument (normally dependent on IPsec or SSL) that verifies the correspondence between a gadget and a safe system, making a safe, scrambled "burrow" over the open web.

• Web security: You should have the option to control the inner staff's web use so as to square electronic dangers from utilizing programs as a vector to contaminate your system.

System security and the cloud

An ever-increasing number of undertakings are offloading a portion of their registering needs to cloud specialist organizations, making half breed foundations where their very own inner system needs to interoperate consistently — and safely — with servers facilitated by third gatherings. In some cases, this framework itself is an independent system, which can be either physical (a few cloud servers cooperating) or virtual (numerous VM cases running together and "organizing" with one another on a solitary physical server).

To deal with the security angles, many cloud merchants set up brought together security control strategies all alone stage. In any case, the stunt here is that those security frameworks won't generally coordinate with your arrangements and methodology for your inside systems, and this confusion can add to the outstanding task at hand for organizing security experts. There is an assortment of devices and systems accessible to you that can help facilitate a portion of this stress, however, in all actuality, this territory is still in transition and the accommodation of the cloud can mean system security cerebral pains for you.

System security programming

To consider every contingency, you'll need an assortment of programming and equipment instruments in your toolbox. Generally admired, as we've noted, is the firewall. The drumbeat has been to state that the days when a firewall was the aggregate of your system security is a distant memory, with guard top to bottom expected to battle dangers behind (and even before) the firewall. Without a doubt, it appears that perhaps the most delightful thing you can say about a firewall item in a survey is that considering it a firewall is undercutting it.

In any case, firewalls can't be caste off totally. They're appropriately one component in your half breed barrier top to bottom technique. Furthermore, as eSecurity Planet clarifies, there are various diverse firewall types, a large number of which map onto the various kinds of system security we secured before:

- Network firewalls

- Next-age firewalls

- Web application firewalls

- Database firewalls

- Unified risk the executives

- Cloud firewalls

- Container firewalls

- Network division firewalls

Past the firewall, a system security ace will convey various apparatuses to monitor what's going on in their systems. A portion of these instruments is corporate items from huge merchants, while others come as free, open-source utilities that sysadmins have been utilizing since the beginning of Unix. An extraordinary asset is SecTools.org, which keeps up a charmingly Web 1.0 site that monitors the most well-known system security apparatuses, as decided on by clients. Top classifications include:

• Packet sniffers, which give profound understanding of information traffic

• Vulnerability scanners like Nessus

• Intrusion location and anticipation programming, similar to the unbelievable Snort

• Penetration testing programming

That last classification may cause a stir — all things considered, what's entrance trying if not an endeavour to hack into a system? In any case, some portion of ensuring you're secured includes perceiving how hard or simple it is to break in, and geniuses know it; moral hacking is a significant piece of system security. That is the reason you'll see instruments like Air crack — which exists to track down remote system security keys — nearby staid corporate contributions that cost countless dollars on the SecTools.org list.

In a situation where you have to get numerous apparatuses to cooperate, you may likewise need to convey SIEM programming, which we addressed previously. SIEM items advanced from logging programming, and dissect arrange information gathered by various devices to recognize suspicious conduct on your system.

System security employments and pay rates

In case you're searching for a vocation in arranging security, you're in karma: these occupations are sought after, and they pay well. Staffing organization

Mondo pegged arrange security investigators as one of the six most lucrative cybersecurity employments, guaranteeing they could gain somewhere in the range of $90,000 and $150,000 per year.

What does a system security expert do, precisely? What's more, is it not the same as a system security engineer? With regards to work titles, there's in every case less clearness than you'd like, as the masters working things out and discussing their vocation ways on this Reddit string exhibit pleasantly.

In principle, a system security engineer is bound to work out security frameworks, while a system security expert is bound to be entrusted with sifting through information from organizing security instruments to discover inconvenience. Yet, actually numerous individuals with the two titles do a tad bit of each, and what you do will pivot more on your expected set of responsibilities than your two-word title. For what it's worth, Glassdoor pegs arrange security investigators as being marginally lower-paid, at around $80K per year instead of $82K for organizing security engineers. Be that as it may, your mileage particularly may differ and you should think about any pay numbers while taking other factors into consideration.)

One thing you can be confident for is that either work is a lifelong way with a future. Alissa Johnson, as of now the CISO of Xerox, was a system security engineer at Northrup Grumman before inevitably ascending the stepping stool into her present official job.

System security affirmations

While there aren't numerous affirmations that attention on arranging security alone, there is a number that can assist you with demonstrating your bona fides, either in light of the fact that they're security confirmations with a system part or a system accreditation that remembers material for security. The absolute most esteemed include:

- CISSP, the "crown gem" of cybersecurity affirmation

- CompTIA's Network+

- Cisco Certified Network Associate

- Certified Ethical Hacker affirmation, for you hopeful infiltration analyzers out there

CHAPTER FIVE
IDENTIFY AND ACCESS MANAGEMENT

Personality and access to the board (IAM) is a system of business procedures, arrangements and innovations that encourages the administration of electronic or advanced characters. With an IAM system set up, data innovation (IT) supervisors can control client access to basic data inside their associations. Personality and access to the board items offer job-based access control, which lets framework managers direct access to frameworks or systems dependent on the jobs of individual clients inside the undertaking.

In this unique circumstance, get to is the capacity of an individual client to play out a particular undertaking, for example, see, make or change a record. Jobs are characterized by work competency, authority and duty inside the venture.

Frameworks utilized for character and access the executives to remember single sign-for frameworks, multifaceted verification and advantaged get to the board (PAM). These innovations additionally give the capacity to safely store character and profile information just as information administration capacities to guarantee that lone information that is fundamental and pertinent is shared. IAM frameworks can be conveyed on-premises, gave by an outsider seller through a cloud-based membership model or sent in a half and half cloud.

Essential parts of IAM

On a major level, IAM includes the accompanying parts:

- How people are recognized in a framework.

- How jobs are recognized in a framework and how they are doled out to people.

- Adding, expelling and refreshing people and their jobs in a framework.

- Assigning levels of access to people or gatherings of people.

- Protecting the touchy information inside the framework and verifying the framework itself.

What IAM frameworks ought to incorporate

The character gets to the board frameworks should comprise of all the fundamental controls and instruments to catch and record client login data, deal with the endeavour database of client personalities and arrange the task and expulsion of access benefits. That implies that frameworks utilized for IAM ought to furnish a brought together index administration with oversight just as permeability into all parts of the organization client base.

Advancements for personality access and the executives ought to streamline the client provisioning and account arrangement process. These frameworks ought to diminish the time it takes to finish these procedures with a controlled work process that diminishes blunders just as the potential for misuse while permitting mechanized record satisfaction. A personality and access to the board framework ought to likewise enable heads to in a split second view and change get to rights.

These frameworks additionally need to adjust the speed and computerization of their procedures with the control that overseers need to screen and change get to rights. Thusly, to oversee get to asks for, the focal registry needs an entrance rights framework that naturally coordinates representative activity titles, specialty unit identifiers and areas to their applicable benefit levels.

Different survey levels can be incorporated as work processes to empower the best possible checking of individual solicitations. This disentangles setting up suitable audit forms for more elevated level access just as facilitating surveys of existing rights to forestall benefit creep, the steady gathering of access rights past what clients need to carry out their responsibilities.

IAM frameworks ought to be utilized to furnish adaptability to build up bunches with explicit benefits for explicit jobs so get to rights dependent on worker work capacities can be consistently appointed. The framework ought to likewise give solicitation and endorsement procedures to changing benefits since workers with a similar title and occupation area may require redid, or somewhat extraordinary, get to.

Advantages of personality and access the board

IAM advancements can be utilized to start, catch, record and oversee client characters and their related access consents in a mechanized way. This brings an association with the accompanying advantages:

• Access benefits are conceded by one translation of approach and all people and administrations are appropriately confirmed, approved and examined.

• Companies that appropriately oversee characters have more prominent control of clients get to, diminishing the danger of inside and outer information breaks.

• Automating IAM frameworks enables organizations to work all the more productively by diminishing the exertion, time and cash that would be required to oversee access to their systems physically.

• In terms of security, the utilization of an IAM system can make it simpler to uphold strategies around client confirmation, approval and benefits, and address issues concerning benefit creep.

• IAM frameworks assist organizations with bettering conform to government guidelines by enabling them to show that corporate data isn't being abused. Organizations can likewise exhibit that any information required for inspecting can be made accessible on request.

Moreover, by executing personality get to the board devices and following related prescribed procedures, an organization can increase a focused edge. For instance, IAM innovations enable the business to give clients outside the association, similar to clients, accomplices, contractual workers, and providers, access to its system crosswise over versatile applications, on-premises applications and programming as-an administration applications without trading off security. This empowers better joint effort, upgraded profitability, expanded proficiency and diminished working expenses.

IAM in the venture

It tends to be trying to get financing for IAM ventures since they don't straightforwardly expand an association's gainfulness or usefulness. Be that as it may, an absence of viable personality and access the board presents noteworthy dangers not exclusively to consistence, yet additionally in general security. These botch issues increment the danger of more noteworthy harms from both outside and interior dangers.

Keeping the necessary progression of business information going while all the while dealing with its entrance has constantly required managerial consideration. The business IT condition is consistently advancing and the troubles have just gotten more prominent with later troublesome patterns like bring your own gadget, distributed computing, versatile applications, and an undeniably portable workforce. There are more gadgets and administrations to be overseen than at any time in recent memory, with various prerequisites for related access benefits.

Dangers related to IAM

Executing legitimate personality and access to the executive's apparatuses or stages implies putting away all approvals and certifications in one, bound together spot. When not verified accurately, this can be a tremendous hazard in such a case that an aggressor accesses the framework, every advanced character can be undermined. Likewise, if a particular work that is approved to the framework doesn't pursue security or secret word best practices, the entirety of the data could be effectively spilled.

Another worry about receiving IAM is difficulties in execution. Heritage frameworks will ordinarily as of now have a personality the board usefulness set up, along these lines, changing over assets to another framework could be testing, costly and tedious. Notwithstanding, answers for limiting the need for specialized help, for example, cloud administrations, are getting progressively reasonable.

IAM sellers and apparatuses

As opposed to creating inner apparatuses, most organizations choose to buy or buy into outsider IAM instruments. These items can take on different structures, for example, a way of life as an assistance (IDAAS) cloud model, a half and half cloud model, a conventional on-premise model or a microservices model. IAM microservices may cover just a single part of IAM like favoured record the executives, account consistence the board or client approval the board.

We as a whole have characters. In the computerized world, our personalities show themselves as characteristics, sections in the database. The inclination for online administrations is to gather these properties so they can serve us better, or make an extraordinary client experience dependent on the information gathered about our static and dynamic qualities.

A one of a kind property separates us from other online clients. Such a trait could be an email address, telephone number, or a standardized savings number. We get traits from our managers as titles, in which specialty unit we have a place with, jobs that we have in ventures, or in the association progressive system. Traits relating to our private and working life are extraordinary and change after some time as we change employments, move, get hitched and so forth.

Character Management

Your online character is built up when you register. During enlistment, a few traits are gathered and put away in the database. The enlistment procedure can be very extraordinary relying upon what sort of advanced personality you will be given. The government provided electronic personality utilizes an extremely intensive procedure, though you can enlist to web-based social networking locales with totally counterfeit (and subsequently unconfirmed) character qualities.

Character the board is tied in with dealing with the qualities. You, your director, your organization HR individual, the IT administrator, the eCommerce site administration work area individual are just a bunch of models who can be liable for making, refreshing, or in any event, erasing ascribes identified with you.

Characteristic = Authorization?

A portion of the personality properties that we have is incredible. They enable us to do things on the web. A job characteristic that depicts a situation inside an organization, a buy chief, for instance, can mention to an online website what the individual is permitted to do on that particular webpage. In this manner, it is very pivotal that credits allowing capacity to the client are deliberately overseen and kept up.

I'm not catching Our meaning By "Access"?

Access choices are Yes/No choices. At the point when an entrance control is sent it will be entrusted with making the Yes/No choice when an online client attempts to enter or utilize the asset. There can be and typically are, various access control focuses inside an online help. On the top level, there's an entrance control guide attempting toward deciding whether the client is permitted to enter the site by any stretch of the imagination. At that point, in the lower level, the entrance control point arrives at the individual records found someplace on the hard drive. A portion of the entrance control focuses is visual to the end client, requiring activities. The most fundamental model would be validation.

What Do We Mean By "Authentication"?

Authentication is a procedure where the individuality of this consumer will be established. There are a lot of different techniques to authenticate the consumer. At the lowest amount the user could assert he knows who he says he's my only writing his title as a reply to the query "Who are you?" On the opposite end of the spectrum that the consumer could sign into the service with his administration issued digital identity (EID). Between both of these examples, you may get a broad selection of distinct procedures and technology for authentication.

Access Administration

So whenever the user identity is established he could get the service? Wrong. Authentication! = Authorization (! = is nerd language and means "not equal"). After authentication that there has to be an access control decision. The choice relies upon the information available in regards to the consumer. This is the point where the characteristics become involved. If the authentication procedure can deliver the essential set of features into the access control choice stage, the procedure can then assess the characteristics and also make the Yes/No choice.

Authorization policy is a tool that can be used to create a formalized decision point. From the realm of Identity and Access Management (IAM), the consent policy could be implemented at a centralized provider, or in the neighbourhood level, or both places. The function of an identity provider would be to perform the heavy lifting of amassing the identity characteristics available and creating the high-level accessibility choices on behalf of internet support. Making an authority policy framework in the service level isn't advisable as it generates complexities, maintenance overhead is difficult to change rapidly and may be error-prone.

The distinction between identity management and access management is so:

    Identity Management is all about managing the characteristics of the consumer
    Access Control is all about assessing the characteristics based on coverages and creating Yes/No decisions

Identity Access Control is a safety area that manages Identity and access privileges for a physical or digital source. IAM ensures the consumer's identity (authentication) and that they can get into the software and tools that they have consent to use (consent).

Why we want IAM? To clearly understand the significance of IAM, first, we look at the way the conventional company infrastructure handles identities and access rights.

According to the standard access management strategy, every program within a company manages the consumer's identity and access rights individually.

Let us know the topics of the approach using a straightforward scenario.

Emma needs to get three internet applications in ABC business according to her demands. But she's to make accounts for every single program with various usernames and passwords.

Identity and Access Management (IAM) applications protect data protection and Solitude beginning with user authentication and authorization, frequently by utilizing one sign-on alternative that integrates multi-factor authentication, then assigns users access rights to sources together with identity management (IDM) solutions to constantly monitor accessibility, to demonstrating enforcement of and governance within "least privilege necessary" access rights.

As authorities and business standards organizations put greater attention on Data privacy and protection, organizations will need to meet stringent compliance requirements. As businesses move mission-critical small business operations into the cloud, strong Identity and Access Management (IAM) helps protect data from unauthorized access. With complicated on-premises, hybrid vehicles, and cloud infrastructures, organizations fight with IAM as more identities -- individual and non-invasive -- interact with info. Identity and Access Control, in its heart, is all about ensuring that the ideal users have the ideal access to the proper tools at the ideal time for the perfect reason.

Which are identity and accessibility?

Identity and accessibility are two elements to the whole of regulating how your customers interact with applications and data across your data systems, databases, networks, and applications.

What's individuality?

Back in the old days, before the cloud, individuality consisted solely of individual users, such as workers or on-premises builders. Digital transformation changes how we define individuality. Nowadays, identity could be an individual, thing, or code which interacts with your own information.

By way of example, an on-premises worker is 1 kind of individuality that presents a certain set of dangers, even though a distant worker is an individuality that introduces another set of dangers. Meanwhile, robotic procedure automation, code that manages administrative jobs, is not the same sort of individuality from a Web of Things (IoT) device.

The proliferation of identities wreaks havoc on IT administrators as everyone wants its own ID and the way to authenticate, in addition to its own set of rights within the ecosystem.

After establishing an identity, You have to ascertain what resources that Individuality may get. By way of instance, every user - whether or not they need access to the tools that let them perform their tasks.

Institutions of higher education offer a Superb example of how accessibility Can become complex. By way of instance, a university professor may hold several identities that need access to unique tools. As teachers, professors want access to sensitive faculty information such as students' grades and advisers. Meanwhile, many colleges also allow staff and faculty to take courses at no cost. As students, professors must just have access to their information, not that of their classmates.

Access can't exist without individuality. But identity is futile without Providing access to sources. Therefore, speaking about one without the other generates an incomplete image.
Which are IAM dangers?

The IAM dangers inherent in contemporary IT infrastructures result in several; Safety, privacy, operational, and compliance risks.

   Best reasons to get started on your Access and Identity Control endeavour

Information security threat

IAM risks grow as businesses produce complex IT infrastructures. By this 2019 Statistics Breach Investigations Report, 34 percent of data breaches involved inner celebrities. Additionally, 15 percent of data breaches involved authorized user privilege misuse. The report detailed that privilege misuse was among the best 3 data breach routines for its Financial and Insurance, Healthcare, Public Administration, Manufacturing, and Retail industries.

Privacy hazard

Although security and privacy are often used interchangeably, they're just two Various kinds of danger. Privacy entails giving individuals control over their personally identifiable information (PII). By way of instance, Human Resources may require access to a worker's medical history. But, that worker has the right to keep the data private from a supervisor. If your organization isn't managing identity and access efficiently, you might be violating somebody's right to privacy.

Operational risk

IAM also protects you from working risks like embezzlement and fraud. Organizations use IAM to handle the Segregation of Duties (SOD). By way of instance, an individual accessing Accounts Receivable shouldn't get Accounts Payable. If the individual can get the person may make a bogus vendor account and cover it in the corporate bank accounts without supervision.

Compliance risk

Based upon Your business, you probably need to Fulfil regulatory compliance requirements. Most regulations require businesses to restrict access to info. By way of instance, under the medical insurance Portability and Accountability Act (HIPAA), a healthcare provider may face penalties ranging from $100 to $50,000 per violation.

GDPR - altering the principles of access and identity management

What's identity handled?

Identity Management (IDM) is how businesses identify, authenticate, and authorize users. IDM focuses on consumer authentication. Simply speaking, authentication guarantees that an individual is who they say they're. Authentication can comprise:

- Unique User Name
- Password
- Multi-Factor Authentication
- Single Sign-On

Problematically, as the business raises the number of assets, you also raise the amount of software to which you have to authorize your customers. As an instance, if you use a shared driveway for cooperation and a revenue enablement tool, then your sales staff members want access to two unique services. As you include more Software-as-a-Service (SaaS) software, you raise the number of resources to which you have to authenticate customers.

Most businesses handle their identity information by creating a warehouse, a huge data repository that includes all ID details. After producing the warehouse they link it to their environments and applications. Should you follow best practices, you want to integrate multi-factor authentication (MFA). MFA requires your customers to utilize multiple of these authentication methods: something that you know (password), something that you have (smartphone, token), or even anything that you are (biometrics).
How is accessibility handled?

Access is a Little different from individuality, but still inherently interconnected. Access defines the tools that an authenticated identity is authorized to use.

Your sales staff, as an example, requires access to collaborative shared drives And sales programs. Your advertising team requires access to collaborative shared drives and advertising software. Nevertheless, your sales staff might not have to get into the advertising software, and the advertising team might not have to get into the revenue software. To complicate access farther, your sales staff might just have to use specific modules inside a marketing program or your marketing staff might just have to use specific modules inside a sales program.

Roles/Groups/Attributes

Included in accessibility management, IT administrators delegate identities functions, Groups, or characteristics that specify the tools users want. As an instance, all sales staff members probably need the same access to the very same resources. To give access separately becomes overpowering for IT administrators so that they make access definitions that aggregate similar users and use those to specify what tools users with these definitions may get. Afterward, when a new user is added who can use that definition, then the IT supplies that individual all of the accessibility needed.

Privileges/Entitlements

IT administrators grant consumers rights, which provides them permission to Access info and the capability to interact with the information.

When we talk about the "Least Privilege Necessary" best practice we imply that You allow an individual to earn the minimum quantity of changes which they will need to perform their tasks. The salesperson may require access to this revenue program and also the ability to modify information.

Problematically, users frequently collect privileges throughout their employment, a phenomenon referred to as "privilege creep" As users move across the organization or socialize with departments aside from their own, they frequently ask access to new tools. While users occasionally must keep this extra accessibility, they frequently only need it for a brief period. But, overburdened IT Managers can get rid of track of if they will need to reverse the accessibility, leaving those users with much more access than they require.

Why is access and identity management important?

Digital transformation alters the safety perimeter, moving it out of Firewalls to individuality. As businesses incorporate new technologies in their business models, they will need to safeguard access and identity more proactively.

In an enterprise-level, you want to concentrate on creating and implementing an IAM Policy that restricts the total amount of data and software with that your identities can socialize. Also, you should broaden your definition of individuality to align with noninvasive identities like robotic procedure automation (RPA), IoT apparatus, service accounts, and programmatic functions.

CHAPTER SIX
SECURITY ASSESSMENT AND TESTING

In today's world, demanding security is not a luxury but a complete necessity. With the introduction of technology, companies have been putting up online infrastructures and, in doing this, have introduced additional goals for the hacking community. Because of this, it's the demand of the hour for community security specialists to do adequate safety evaluation and testing.

CISSP (certified information systems security professional) certificate is Among the main information security certificates in the world and its security evaluation and analyzing as an essential part of its own CBK. The goals of the article include speaking about the concepts of safety evaluation and analyzing CISSP aspirants should be familiar with, together with high-quality overviews of these strategies, testing procedures, and operational controls a safety enforcer ought to know about.

WHAT IS SECURITY ASSESSMENT AND TESTING?

As the name implies, safety evaluation is the process of assessing the Security criteria of a system. Throughout the procedure, we inspect the machine for any probable vulnerabilities, risks, or dangers. The majority of the time, analyzing the safety entails the following measures:

- Requirement analysis and scenario analysis
- Safety policy creation and upgrade

- Document inspection
- Risk identification
- Vulnerability scan
- Data investigation
- Report & briefing

More info about the issue is available here.

1 example of a safety evaluation can function as an open internet application security Job (OWASP), which may be employed to check a system against a number of the most frequent threats introduced to systems hosted on the net. More details and the comprehensive testing manual are available here.

Security Assessment and CISSP

Many certificates need an aspirant to become considerably well-versed with all the safety evaluation and testing methods and/or criteria; the CISSP certification is not any different. (ISC)2's motto, "Inspiring a protected and secure cyber world" wouldn't be warranted if they did not pay sufficient attention to the requirement for complex safety testing acumen.

To be adequately prepared for the fifth domain name of the CISSP exam, an aspirant must:

- Know the unique international legal difficulties.
- Understand different investigative techniques.
- Know, and be able to practically implement forensic processes.
- Know the dangers and vulnerabilities that may be within a generic system.
- Be well-versed in handling third party governance.

POSSIBLE THREATS

Out of the numerous dangers that have to be catered to, here are some of the most frequent ones:

The elevation of privilege attack:

At a privilege elevation attack, a hacker does just what the title of this Attack indicates: elevates their rights on a system, out of, say, "User" to "Administrator." This may be prevented by the implementation of occasionally upgraded ACLs (access control lists).

URL manipulation:

URL manipulation is among the simplest methods to hack a system also, even though the majority of the systems nowadays are vulnerable to these attacks, there are a few vulnerable infrastructures that could be retrieved via manipulation of this URL. To avert this, network engineers will need to execute rigorous authentication and/or consent methods.

Denial of service:

A denial of service (DOS) attack produces a machine or some other source of a system inaccessible to the licensed administrative personnel. All these are really sophisticated strikes and decent care has to be taken to stop these from occurring. More details could be read here.

Spoofing of individuality:

In this attack, a hacker impersonates a legitimate user of a system to Gain access to significant resources on a system.

SECURITY TESTING Methods

We cannot apply complete security on a system but If adequate security evaluation tests are conducted, they could go a long way toward ensuring the machine is free of their very basic vulnerabilities that could be found in the system structure. Few of the methods are:

Ethical hacking:

Not all of the hackers in the world are despicable; the white-hat or moral Hackers are individuals with exemplary hacking wisdom using their art to detect potential flaws in a system. An ethical hacker attempts to bypass the safety of a system utilizing the most sophisticated strategies and resources, but just to locate the probable vulnerabilities in a method.

Penetration testing:

Penetration testing is just another technique in which an instrument (or a specialist) attempts to penetrate the machine via the community to learn possible issues of attack. More on the subject here.

Load testing:

Load testing of a system also needs to be achieved before making it live. This type of procedure, a method is analyzed with the utmost (anticipated) load and its performance is judged. A good illustration may be sending multiple thousand requests to a host concurrently to look at its efficacy.

This Detailed OWASP manual on safety testing could be consulted for more details regarding the situation.

THE APPROACH

To get ready for safety testing, the following strategy can be obtained:

- The analysis of this security structure should be the very first step. Within this measure, the company requirements, goals and safety aims have to be understood concerning the company's security compliance.
- The security structure has to be examined.
- After examined, we will need to classify safety testing. This measure involves collecting the machine installation data that was utilized to create network and software issues (e.g., hardware, engineering, and operating systems, etc.). Pen down the security risks and vulnerabilities found.
- A danger profile today has to be made to simulate the dangers.
- When the threat was identified along with the vulnerabilities discovered, execute the preparation of this exam plan to cater to your issues and/or dangers.
- A traceability matrix has to be made for every single danger, vulnerability, and safety risk.
- At this point, if you demand a tool to execute the testing (tools have been cited in the subsequent section), select it wisely and use it to test.
- Prepare the situation document for the safety tests.
- Execute the test instances.
- Prepare a comprehensive report indicating the forms of threats, vulnerabilities, and risks discovered, together with specifics of how they have been dealt with.

TOOLS TO USE

The most exquisite safety testing programs are:

BeEF:

The Browser Exploitation Framework is a motor that uses a browser to Infiltrate a method. It'll run on Linux, Apple MAC OS X, and Windows operating systems.

Brakeman:

An open-source vulnerability scanner, the brakeman was created especially for Ruby on Rails software. It will aid a programmer test code to find safety problems. Stop by the site to acquire more details.

Nikto:

Nikto is a web server scanner that can help detect incorrect information and Obsolete applications configurations (among other items) that are operating or current on a host. It may be employed to carry out detailed evaluations on servers.

Oedipus:

An open-minded, OS-independent web-app safety (testing and analysis) Package, Oedipus may be used to parse several types of logs (off-site) to discover security vulnerabilities and hazards.

Paros:

Paros is an HTTP/HTTPS proxy written in Java that can be used to locate possible vulnerabilities within a web program. The scanners may intercept (and change) all of the information between clients and servers, such as cookies and form fields.

Vulnerability assessments normally fall into one of 3 classes:

· Personnel testing: Reviews regular practices and processes that consumers follow.

· Physical testing: Reviews centre and midsize protections.

· Network and system testing: Reviews programs, apparatus, and network topology.

The security analyst who'll be doing a vulnerability assessment needs to Know the devices and systems which are on the community and the tasks that they perform. The analyst requires this information to have the ability to evaluate the vulnerabilities of these devices and systems based on the known and possible dangers to the systems and apparatus.

After gaining knowledge about the systems and systems, the safety analyst Should examine present controls in place and establish any threats from those controllers. The safety analyst may then use all of the information gathered to ascertain which automated instruments to use to seek out vulnerabilities. Following the vulnerability investigation is finished, the safety analyst must confirm the results to make certain they are accurate and then report the findings into management, together with hints for remedial actions. With this info in hand, the analyst must execute threat modelling to recognize the dangers that could adversely impact systems and apparatus and also the assault methods that may be utilized.

Vulnerability evaluation programs include Nessus, Open Vulnerability Assessment System (OpenVAS), Core Impact, Nexpose, GFI Langured, Qualys Guard, and Microsoft Baseline Security Analyzer (MBSA). Of those programs, OpenVAS and MBSA are liberated.

When Choosing a vulnerability assessment tool, you need to research the Following metrics: precision, reliability, scalability, and coverage. Truth is the most important metric. A false positive normally leads to time spent exploring a problem that doesn't exist. A false negative is much more serious because it indicates that the scanner failed to recognize a problem that poses a severe safety threat.

Network Discovery Scan

A system discovery scan assesses an assortment of IP addresses to ascertain that ports are available. This sort of scan simply shows a listing of programs on the network as well as the ports being used on the system. It doesn't really look after any vulnerabilities.

Topology discovery involves determining the apparatus in the system, their Connectivity connections to one another, as well as the inner IP addressing scheme being used. Any mixture of those pieces of data enables a user to make a "map" of this system, which assists him tremendously in assessing and interpreting the information he collects in different areas of the hacking procedure. When he's fully successful, he'll get a diagram of this community. Your challenge as a safety practitioner is to ascertain if such a mapping method is possible, using the very same tools as the attacker. According to your findings, you need to determine the action to take that produce topology discovery more difficult or, even better, hopeless.

Operating system fingerprinting is the process of using a method to determine the operating system running on a server or a host. By identifying the OS version and build number, a hacker could identify common vulnerabilities of the OS using easily available documentation in the net. Though lots of the problems will have been addressed in subsequent upgrades, service packs, and hotfixes, there could be zero-day flaws (problems that have never been widely treated or treated by the seller) that the consumer could leverage at the assault. Furthermore, if some of the appropriate security patches have never been implemented, the flaws that the stains were meant to address will exist on the device. As a result, the role of trying OS fingerprinting during evaluation is to evaluate the comparative ease by which it could be achieved and identifying approaches to make it even more difficult.

Operating systems have renowned vulnerabilities and thus do common services. By deciding the services which are working on a platform, an attacker finds potential vulnerabilities of this support of which he can try to make the most. This is generally done using a port scan, were "open," or "listening," vents are identified. Yet more, the lion's share of those difficulties will have been interfering with the correct security patches, but that's not necessarily the case; it isn't unusual for safety analysts to discover that systems that are running vulnerable services are still overlooking the appropriate security patches. Therefore, when performing support discovery, assess patches on systems utilized to have open ports. It's likewise a good idea to close any vents not mandatory for the machine to perform its job.

Network discovery tools may perform the following kinds of scans:

· TCP SYN scan: Sends a packet to every scanned port together with the SYN flag set. When a reply is obtained together with the SYN and ACK flags set, the vent is open.

· TCP ACK scan: Sends a packet to every port using the ACK flag set. If no reply is obtained, then the port is indicated as filtered. When an RST answer is obtained, then the port is indicated as unfiltered.

· Christmas scan: Sends a packet with the FIN, PSH, and URG flags set. If the interface is open, there's absolutely no response. If the interface is shut, the target responds with an RST/ACK package.

The result of the type of scan is that safety professionals can ascertain If vents are open, closed, or filtered. Open ports are used by an application on the remote system. Closed ports are available vents but there's not any application requiring connections on this port. Filtered ports are ports that can't be achieved.

The most frequently used network detection scanning instrument is Nmap.

Network Vulnerability Scan

Network vulnerability scans play a more complicated scan of this network than Network discovery scans.

These scans will probe a concentrated system or network to identify vulnerabilities. The resources used in this kind of scan will have a record of known vulnerabilities and will determine whether a particular vulnerability is present on each apparatus.

There are two kinds of vulnerability scanners:

· Passive vulnerability scanners: A passive vulnerability scanner (PVS) monitors network traffic at the packet layer to ascertain topology, services, and vulnerabilities. It avoids the uncertainty which may be introduced into some system by actively scanning for vulnerabilities.

PVS tools examine the packet flow and look for Vulnerabilities through immediate analysis. They're deployed in substantially the exact same manner as intrusion detection systems (IDSs) or packet analyzers. A PVS can select a network session that targets a secure server and track it as far as required. The biggest advantage of a PVS is the capacity to perform its work without affecting the monitored network. A few examples of PVSs would be the Nessus Network Monitor (previously Tenable PVS) and NetScan tools Pro.

· Lively vulnerability scanners: Whereas passive scanners may simply collect information, active exposure scanners (AVSs) can take actions to block an attack, like block a harmful IP address. They may also be used to simulate an assault to evaluate readiness. They function by sending transmissions and analyzing the answers. Due to this, these scanners can disrupt traffic. Examples include Nessus and Microsoft Baseline Security Analyzer (MBSA).

Irrespective of whether it is passive or active, a vulnerability scanner can't replace the experience of trained safety personnel. Furthermore, these scanners are just as powerful as the signature databases where they rely on, hence the databases have to be updated frequently. At length, scanners demand bandwidth and possibly slow down the system.

For best performance, you can put a vulnerability scanner at a subnet that needs to be shielded. You could even join a scanner through a firewall for numerous subnets; this disrupts the setup and necessitates opening ports on the firewall, which might be problematic and may affect the functioning of the firewall.

The hottest network vulnerability scanning programs comprise Qualys, Nessus, and MBSA.

Web Application Vulnerability Scan

Because web applications are highly utilized in the world today, businesses need to make sure their web applications remain protected and free from vulnerabilities. Web application vulnerability scanners are specific tools that analyze web applications for known vulnerabilities.

Popular internet application vulnerability scanners comprise QualysGuard and Nexpose.
Penetration Testing

The Objective of penetration testing, also called ethical hacking, is to simulate an assault to recognize any dangers that could stem from internal or external sources intending to exploit the vulnerabilities of a machine or apparatus.

NIST SP 800-92

NIST SP 800-92 makes these recommendations for more efficient and effective log management:

- Organizations need to establish policies and processes for log management. Included in this preparation procedure, a company must surpass its logging demands and goals.
    - Create policies that clearly define mandatory requirements and proposed recommendations for log management actions.
    - Make sure that applicable policies and processes incorporate and encourage log management demands and guidelines.
    - Management must offer essential support for those attempts between log management planning, policy, and process development.
- Organizations must prioritize log direction appropriately throughout the business.
- Organizations must produce and keep a log management infrastructure.
- Organizations must offer appropriate support for all employees with log management duties.
- Organizations should set conventional log direction functional procedures. Including ensuring that administrators
    - Monitor the logging status of log resources.
    - Monitor log spinning and archival procedures.

- Assess for updates and patches to logging applications and get, test, and deploy them.
- Make sure that every logging server's clock is synchronized to a frequent time source.
- Reconfigure logging as required according to policy changes, technology changes, and other elements.
- Document and document anomalies in log configurations, settings, and procedures.

According Into NIST SP 800-92, shared log management infrastructure elements consist of general purposes (log parsing, event filtering, and event aggregation), storage (log rotation, log archival, log loss, log conversion, log normalization, and log file integrity checking), log analysis (event correlation, log viewing, and log coverage), and also log disposal (log clearing.)

Syslog provides an easy framework for log entrance creation, storage, and transport that any operating system, security applications, or program could use if made to do so. Many log resources use Syslog because of their native logging arrangement or provide characteristics that enable their log formats to be converted into Syslog format. Every Syslog message has just 3 components. The first part defines the severity and facility as numerical values. The next area of the message includes a timestamp along with the hostname or IP address of the origin of the log. The next part is the real log message content.

No standard fields are described inside the content material; it is meant to be human-readable rather than readily machine-parable. This provides very large flexibility for log generators, which may put whatever information they deem significant inside the content area, but it creates an automatic evaluation of the log information quite challenging. A single source can use many unique formats because of its log message material, so an investigation program would have to be familiarized with every single format and also have the ability to extract the significance of the information within the fields of every format. This issue becomes even harder when log messages are created by many resources. It may not be possible to comprehend the significance of all log messages; therefore investigation may be limited to pattern and keyword searches. Some organizations designing their Syslog infrastructures so that similar kinds of messages have been grouped or delegated similar principles, which may make log evaluation automation much easier to carry out.

As log safety is now a larger concern, many implementations of Syslog are established that put greater emphasis on safety. Many are based on IETF's RFC 3195, which has been created especially to enhance the safety of Syslog. Implementations according to this standard can encourage log confidentiality, integrity, and accessibility through several attributes, such as dependable log shipping, transmission confidentiality security, and transmission integrity protection and authentication.

Safety Data and event management (SIEM) products enable administrators to Consolidate all safety information logs. This consolidation guarantees that administrators can analyze most of the logs from one source rather Than needing to test every log onto its separate source. Most SIEM Solutions Support two means of collecting logs from log generators:

Agentless: The SIEM server receives information from the respective hosts without having to possess any particular software installed on these hosts. Some servers pull logs out of the hosts, which is generally done with the server authenticate to each server and recover its logs frequently. In other scenarios, the hosts drive their logs into the host, which generally entails every host reverted to the server and shifting its own logs frequently. Irrespective of whether the logs are either pulled or pushed, the host then performs event filtering and aggregation and log normalization and analysis on the collected logs.

Agent-based: A broker application is installed on the server to do event filtering and aggregation and log normalization for a special sort of log. The server then transmits the normalized log information to the SIEM server, normally on a real-time or near-real-time foundation for storage and analysis. Numerous agents might have to be installed if your server has multiple kinds of logs of attention. Some SIEM goods also offer brokers for generic formats like Syslog and Easy Network Management Protocol (SNMP). A universal agent is utilized primarily to find log information from a source where a format-specific broker and an agentless system aren't offered. Some products also enable administrators to create customized brokers to manage unsupported log resources.

You will find benefits and disadvantages to each method. The main benefit of this agentless approach is that brokers don't have to be set up, configured, and maintained on every logging host. The main drawback is the absence of filtering and aggregation in the individual server level, which may cause considerably larger quantities of information to be moved over networks and raise the quantity of time that it takes to filter and then examine the logs.

Another possible drawback of this agentless method is the SIEM server might require qualifications for authenticating to every logging server. Sometimes, just one of both approaches is achievable; for instance, there could not be a way to collect logs from a certain server without having an agent onto it.

SIEM Products generally consist of support for many dozen kinds of log sources, like OSs, security applications, software servers (e.g., internet servers, email servers), as well as physical safety management devices like badge readers. For every supported log supply kind, except for generic formats like Syslog, the SIEM products usually understand how to categorize the many crucial logged fields. This considerably boosts the normalization, evaluation, and significance of log information over that conducted by applications using a less granular comprehension of particular log formats and sources. Additionally, the SIEM applications can do occasion decrease by disregarding data areas that aren't important to computer safety, possibly decreasing the SIEM applications' network bandwidth and data storage utilization.

Typically, System, system, and security administrators are accountable for handling logging on their programs, executing routine analysis of the log data, reporting and recording the outcomes of the log management tasks, and also ensuring that log information is offered to the log management infrastructure in accord with the company's policies. Additionally, a number of their organization's safety administrators behave as log-in infrastructure administrators, together with duties like the following:

Contact system-level administrators to acquire extra information about an event or to ask that they explore a specific occasion.

Identify changes necessary to system logging settings (e.g., which entrances and information fields are routed to the cantered log servers, what log format ought to be utilized) and notify system-level administrators of those vital alterations.

Initiate answers to events, such as episode handling and operational issues (e.g., a collapse of a log management infrastructure element).

Make sure that old log information is archived to removable media and disposed of correctly after it's no more desired.

Cooperate with requests from legal counsel, auditors, and many others.

Monitor the condition of the log management infrastructure (e.g., failures in logging applications or log archival networking, failures of local systems to move their log info) and initiate appropriate answers when issues happen.

Evaluation and execute upgrades and upgrades to the log management infrastructure's components.

Keep the safety of this log management infrastructure.

Organizations should create policies that clearly define mandatory requirements and proposed recommendations for many facets of log management, such as log production, log transmission, log storage, and disposal, and log analysis. Table 6-3 gives illustrations of logging configuration preferences that a company can utilize. The kinds of values described in Table 6-3 should just be put on the hosts and server elements previously given by the business as ones that need to or if log security-related occasions.

CHAPTER SEVEN
SECURITY OPERATIONS

INTRODUCTION

Cybercrime is growing exponentially every year, together with the Yearly global Price Of these offenses now approaching over $100 billion. An estimated 13 million documents are vulnerable every year from a mixture of viruses, malware, phishing, Web-based strikes, and malevolent insider activities, and roughly 35 percent of attacks target companies.

Cybercriminals today are targeting associations of all sizes -- notably Huge associations since they have an extensive footprint and given the character of the information in their networks that make them a tempting target for cybercriminals. To protect business-critical IT and business infrastructure against these cyber offenders, deploying a comprehensive security tracking infrastructure and constructing a Security Operations Centre (SOC) is vital.

Security operations are worried about the daily access and safety of System tools. This usually means that there has to be a Security Operations centre (SOC) frame set up composed of the correct policies, criteria, guidelines, and procedures for the heart and assistance services of a company. The policies should also be under continuous review to ensure they stay current and relevant. Using these policies in place, and reviewing them as essential, a company is showing due diligence and care. Securing a system constantly requires walking a fine line between ensuring customers have access to the resources and tools required to execute their tasks while protecting the community.

1 area of concern to the operational staff is in supplying high Accessibility. During RAID, clustering, and redundant alternatives, a company can decrease downtime, if the problems are a consequence of a malicious attack or only a potential failure.

Also, among the key areas from the safety operations is appropriate storage and Entry methods. All these are part of regular operation processes. What's more, system management, configuration management, and change management are duties of surgeries too. Tasks under centre solutions also include penetration testing, vulnerability assessments as well as the execution of IDS/IPS controls to supply another layer of confidence in the community.

The Security Operations domain name for CISSP mostly focuses on discovering and Protecting sensitive and business-critical data in any business. There are many core safety operations versions briefly touched upon that any company should follow to provide complete security protection to a company.

When we think about the word "operations" we normally consider the daily tasks essential to conduct a small business. Therefore that the expression Security Operations revolves around ensuring that we've got policies, criteria, processes, etc., set up to make sure that our regular business functions are protected and that we are supplying Confidentiality, Integrity, and Availability (C-I-A) into the regular functions of the enterprise.

Resource protection makes sure that websites and other resources that are Beneficial to the company are safeguarded throughout this source. The objective of Patch and Vulnerability Management would be to identify controls and procedures that will offer proper protection against dangers that could adversely impact the safety of the data system or information entrusted to the data system. Successful implementation of those controls will make a continuously configured environment that's protected against known vulnerabilities in the operating system and application program. The objective of the Incident Management plan is to set up controls and procedures that will offer the company's data system's effective tracking capacity and responsiveness against security threats and events. The design and execution of an event management frame can secure the data system against known vulnerabilities and risks.

The main objectives for CISSP comprise:

- Recognizing safety operations theories
    - Need-to-know/least privilege
    - Separation of duties and responsibilities
    - Monitor unique privileges (e.g., operators, administrators)
    - Job spinning
    - Marking, managing, preserving, and destroying sensitive data
    - Record retention
- Implementing resource security
    - Media management
- Care and performance of IT Security Assets & Services
    - Asset management (e.g., gear life cycle, software licensing)
    - Safety Operations centre

- Vulnerability Management
- Endpoint Protection
- Data Security
- Proxy and Internet Content Filtering
- Network Forensics
- Information Risk Management
- Change and Configuration Management (versioning, baselines, etc.)

Control Layers

The key points that CISSP concentrates on deriving the safety operations Comprise:

Info owners must dictate that can access funds and how much ability users may have. The security manager's job is to be certain that occurs.

Administrative, physical, and technical controls must be used to attain the management's directives.

Administrative controls include publication and development of policies, criteria, processes, and guidelines; screening of employees; safety awareness training; and monitoring of system action and change control processes.
Instance: Strategies indicating how servers must be set up, annual safety awareness instruction for all workers, implementing a change control application.

Technical controls include logical access control mechanisms, resource and password management, identification and authentication procedures, security apparatus and setup of their system.
Instance: Anti-virus applications, intrusion detection methods, locking down working systems, encryption, firewalls.

Physical controls involve controlling human entry to the centre and unique sections, locking methods and eliminating unnecessary floppy or CD-ROM drives, protecting the perimeter of the centre, monitoring for intrusion and ecological controls.

Instance: Eliminating floppy drives in computers, locking system, safety guards monitoring the centre, ac and humidity control.

The data owner is generally a senior executive over the direction group of the provider. The data owner has the ultimate company duty of information protection and is the one held accountable for any neglect in regards to protecting the organization's information resources. The individual that holds this function is accountable for assigning a classification to this data and dictating how the data ought to be guarded.

If the data owner doesn't lay out the base of data security and be sure that the directives have been enforced, this could violate the due care idea.

Access Control Types

There are lots of kinds of security mechanisms and they need to function together. The complexity of the controls and also of the surroundings they're in may cause the controllers to contradict each other or leave gaps in safety. This may introduce unforeseen holes at the organization's protection which aren't fully known from the implementers.

Really strict technical access controls may be set up and all of the Mandatory administrative controls might be up to snuff, but when any individual is permitted to access every system at the centre, then you will find definite security dangers present inside the environment.

Directive Controls are particulate coverages to preclude or mandate activities to decrease risk. All controls which are administrative, physical or technical can be readily sub-categorized as preventative, corrective or detective.
Technical next-generation concentrate places - Threat Intelligence, evaluation, and other safety operation services

Some of the major focus areas to mitigate the cyber safety risks to any Business from a specialized safety agency are:

Threat and event investigation

    Security awake evaluation, notification, and escalation, 24/7/365
   Tips for remediation
    Trend evaluation and coverage in regularly scheduled intervals (weekly, monthly, and quarterly)

System service and health tracking

   Operational evaluation and recommendations
   Supply information feed tracking

Threat Intelligence

   Threat analysis and research solutions

Threat intelligence (hazard study and evaluation)

Almost as important as understanding what safety events are occurring or have taken place is your capability to understand what emerging security dangers may directly affect your company in the not too distant future. Here is the aim of safety performance solutions, which includes a package of solutions (like investigations, analysis types, logging and tracking, protected provisioning, resource security methods, event management, preventative steps, etc.), offering:

Enriched threat intellect feeds that can be incorporated into the company's deployed Safety Incident and Event Management (SIEM) solution to allow correlation of security incidents at the business's infrastructure together with known poor actors in the wild. While the reach of the proposed campaign does not include investigations that are depending upon the alarms which get triggered through these feeds integration into SIEM, the safety operation analysts will track information that is incorporated in the SIEM surroundings.

Threat brains use content and case management, which implements custom and generic threat intelligence tracking content in organizations tracking the surroundings. While the reach of services doesn't normally constitute pruning of their SIEM for almost any business's environment, the safety analysts will identify pruning needs during the job and adhere to the change management procedure to have it aligned to the company and deployed at the infrastructure.

The hazard analysis and research solutions offer the analysts working with a company's security tracking team the accessibility to company insights to have a detailed hazard analysis corresponding to this business enterprise. This enables interactive analysis and research about current and emerging dangers providing business contextualization.

The clarified security services empower analysts to cross-reference alerts And events with possibly known bad actors, that will significantly boost the Security Operations centre's (SOC) capability to innovate and supply recommendations and analysis into the business enterprise. Furthermore, periodic inspections of the safety procedures and hazard analysis and research are crucial to mature the procedures and to recognize possible emerging priority dangers for a company.
System assistance and health observation (operational evaluation and system health)

Of equal significance to alerting and reporting on safety events are the Continuous review of episodes after the fact to indicate short- and - long-term improvements to a company's response position. To this end, the SOC should incorporate an operational evaluation element, which cross-analyses a broad spectrum of alarms to search for comprehensive indicators of systemic safety and/or SIEM operational difficulties.

The operational evaluation Ought to Be performed in parallel with additional Monitoring places and need no interruption of those services. Security analysts must examine an aggregation of their organization's alarms, reports, and customer feedback. The outcome of the Procedure is regular checkpoints straight back into the company emphasizing:

- Possible security problems
- Potential security infrastructure misconfigurations or necessary spots

- Suggested improvements to a company's incident response processes
- Suggested improvements to present SIEM content
- Added SIEM content for present use cases
- Added use cases to address issues identified through operational evaluation

The operational evaluation provides weekly and daily reporting on the Company's L2/L3 incident response group, punctuated by monthly review meetings where the safety analyst facilitates a comprehensive discussion of the safety trends identified from episode analysis over its foundation, by way of instance the previous month. The operational evaluation service may also leverage hazard research to give perspective on evolving risks that could impact a company's security infrastructure and operations.

The focus on provisioning system health care services is Vital in the Security systems analysts will, at regular intervals, review the patch levels and system accessibility of the company's security tracking infrastructure. For systems that need patching or hardening, the analyst may input a ticket at the reporting system and follow up with the right stakeholder to verify that required patches are implemented or monitoring detectors that have undergone an outage have been restored to service. The analyst will aggregate the tickets for addition to the surgeries investigation report.

In doing the machine wellness services, the safety team should leverage a value-added, predefined procedure for making sure that the SIEM source apparatus are reporting in the SIEM as anticipated. This procedure ought to be developed and assessed as a consequence of tracking company infrastructure within a company and should include the creation of a weekly overview of variances from anticipated reporting.

CHAPTER EIGHT
SOFTWARE DEVELOPMENT SECURITY

The Range of program development has improved considerably over the past few years. Since the program environment has become more complicated and hard, the outcome is a more threat-prone environment where safety is the fundamental element in the effective implementation of a program.

The software can have security vulnerabilities that Might Have Been introduced Intentionally or unintentionally by programmers. That is the reason why hardware and software controllers are required, even though they might not necessarily prevent difficulties stemming from programming. As an essential part of the software development process, safety is a continuous process that involves practices and people that jointly guarantee the confidentiality, integrity, and reliability of a program.

Let Us Examine the software development safety criteria and the way that we can Verify the development of protected software.
What Systems Development Controls can I want to know for the CISSP exam?

Systems development is a series of measures for creating, changing, or keeping a company's information system. System development may be utilized in various ways for example:

A procedure or a set of formal tasks employed for creating a new or changing a present information system.

A record specifying a methods development process called the systems development criteria manual.

A life cycle demonstrating the development and maintenance of data systems from beginning till the execution and its constant use.

From the context of this third possibility Mentioned Previously, systems development can also be known as systems development life cycle or application development life cycle (SDLC). From a safety standpoint, software programmers who create the code for a program have to embrace a vast selection of secure programming techniques. At each level of this internet application-like user interface, logic, control, database, etc., safety needs to be an intrinsic component. But most programmers don't understand safe coding practices and the frameworks they use frequently lack critical core controllers that aren't protected by default. Failing to appeal to this software development safety record, programmers frequently lose in the sport of safety when developing software programs.

OWASP Top Ten Proactive Controls 2016 provides a listing of techniques that must be included for application development safety. This program development security record enlists the controllers in order of priority, beginning from the main control.

- Confirm for a safety early and frequently.
- Parameterize questions.
- Encode data.
- Validate all input signals.
- Employ identity and authentication controls.

- Employ appropriate access controllers.
- Shield data.
- Employ logging and intrusion detection.
- Leverage safety frameworks and libraries.
- Error and exception handling.

High-Level Review (SDLC, Versions, PERT, Software Testing)

Previously, organizations were largely focused on producing, releasing, and maintaining operational applications. Now, however, as safety issues and related business risks have grown, they're paying more attention to the integration of safety into the application development procedure.

The Software Development Life Cycle (SDLC) and the CISSP

This is a framework that defines the procedure of building a software application or program from its model to the end merchandise. Generally, SDLC may be divided up into the following stages:

- Planning and demand gathering -- company requirements are assembled.
- Architecture and Design -- software and system design are ready in line with the requirements gathered from the initial stage.
- Evaluation Planning -- and evaluation approach is determined to make a decision as to what to examine and how to check.
- Coding and Coding -- programming is carried out by dividing system layout into performing modules.

- Testing and Deployment -- that the developed product is tested from the real requirements to check it serves the goal.
- Release and Maintenance -- that the last product is discharged and period to time upkeep is done in order to repair problems that come up.

Software Development Life Cycle Models Covered around the CISSP

Let's take examine six fundamental SDLC models and the way they work.

Waterfall Model -- Here is the earliest and most frequent version employed for SDLC methodology. It functions on the principle of completing one stage and then continuing on to another one. Every phase builds upon data collected from the last phase and contains another project program. Even though it's not hard to handle, delays in 1 stage can impact the entire project deadline. Additionally, once a stage is finished, there's very little space for alterations before the job reaches the upkeep period.

V-Shaped Model -- This version is also called the confirmation and validation version. It's comparable to the waterfall model, however with every stage there's a corresponding testing stage too.

Iterative Model -- This version relies on reproduction and improvement. As opposed to developing applications based upon fully known demands, a set of requirements has been implemented, tested, and executed. According to additional requirements and proposed improvements, a new variant or iterative version of the program is made until the final product is complete. The best thing about this version is a fundamental working version could be made early but its drawback is it can quickly consume your resources due to repeat of this procedure.

Spiral Model -- A very flexible version for SDLC, this functions on the principle of this iterative version by replicating four phases over and over at a spiral, allowing for progress with every round. This version may lead to customized merchandise.

Big Bang Model -- This version doesn't work on any particular process. It's only acceptable for smaller jobs; few funds are spent on preparation whilst bulk are spent on growth.

Agile Model -- The most agile version is based on client interaction and opinions. It divides the merchandise into cycles and provides a functioning product as a continuing discharge with incremental adjustments from the preceding cycle. The item is analyzed with every iteration.

Preventing SDLC: Why Is It Important?

Until today, applications engineers have embraced a test-after-completion plan to detect security-related problems in applications. This strategy hasn't been effective, as it contributes to issues that are either found too late or so are left undiscovered. By incorporating safety practices across the SDLC, we could identify and reduce vulnerabilities sooner in every stage, thus creating a stronger and more secure software program.

A Safe SDLC procedure incorporates crucial security modules like code Evaluation, penetration testing, and structure investigation into the full process from start to finish. It not only leads to a more protected product but in addition, it allows early detection of vulnerabilities in the program. This then helps decrease costs by solving problems as they arise, and in addition, it mitigates possible organizational dangers that could arise from an insecure program.

A protected SDLC is normally installed by introducing safety actions to an already present SDLC procedure, e.g., running design danger analysis throughout the design phase of SDLC

Below, a few of the suggested Secure SDLC versions are explained briefly.

   Microsoft Security Development Life Cycle (MS SDL) -- This version was suggested by Microsoft and operates on the principle of procuring the Basic stages of SDLC
   NIST 800-64 -- This gives safety concerns in the information systems development life cycle. It assists businesses to construct safety in their IT development procedures.
   Comprehensive Lightweight Application Security Process (CLASP) -- that is made up of a set of procedures mapped to project roles and enables software developers to construct security into the first phases of SDLC.

Program Evaluation Review Technique (PERT)

A PERT chart is a tool used by project managers for monitoring, organizing, and organizing project tasks. It reduces the time and costs of a job. It's a tool for controlling and planning by management and may be thought of as a roadmap of a job where all significant events have been identified, together with their corresponding components.

Among the fundamental elements of PERT is the identification of crucial activities on which other tasks rely also referred to as the critical path method or CPM.

PERT evaluation is symbolized with the Support of a network structure which suggests all project actions, their interrelation, and also the sequence where they have to be completed.

Concerning software development safety, PERT is utilized to review the magnitude of a software product being designed and also execute hazard assessment by calculating the standard deviation. By estimating maximum potential dimensions, most likely dimensions and lowest potential dimensions, PERT provides recommendations for improvement to application developers to create more efficient applications. With progress created with the assistance of PERT, the real size of this software produced needs to be smaller.

Software Testing and the CISSP

Software testing is a procedure used to detect bugs in applications by executing an application or an application. Additionally, it intends to confirm that the program functions as expected and matches with the technical and business needs, as intended from the design and development period.

Software testing could be run statically or dynamically. In a static Evaluation, flaws are found without executing the code; i.e., through files inspection, source code review, etc...

In a dynamic evaluation, the code has been implemented to inspect the effect of the test. This is performed through the validation procedure, e.g., integration testing, unit testing, etc.

Testing applications for safety is integral to construction application reliability and reputation. It will help identify any vulnerabilities or bugs and sees if the program could be hacked without consent. It assesses the ability and behavior of applications in times of malicious assault and decides whether an information system may protect data or keep the planned functionality. Software security testing should check the six fundamental theories of confidentiality, integrity, availability, authentication, authorization, and non-repudiation.

Storing Data and Information

Storing information and information safely prevents unauthorized people or Parties from accessing it and averts deliberate or unintentional destruction of this data. When creating applications, it's very important to take into account where the data accessed by the program is going to be composed, read, tracked, or shared. The procedures which will be utilized for saving, modifying, transmitting, or displaying information and data are all resources that have to be correctly secured.

Which Exactly Are Knowledge-Based Systems?

A knowledge-based system is a computer system that creates and uses knowledge derived from several sources of information and data. It utilizes artificial intelligence to address complicated issues and helps to encourage humans in decision making and in taking a variety of actions. Decisions made by knowledge-based systems derive from the data stored inside them, which permits them to comprehend complex conditions and process the information accordingly.

Knowledge-based systems are classified into intelligent tutoring systems, CASE-based systems, expert systems, hypertext manipulation, and intelligent user interfaces. The system normally is made up of a knowledge base and an engine. The port engine is the same as a search engine, although the knowledge base is a repository of knowledge.

When we compare knowledge-based methods to computer-based data systems, There are lots of benefits. They can take care of a decent number of unstructured information and provide efficient info. They're also able to examine stored information and economically create new knowledge from it.

Knowledge-based systems in protected software development can let developers categorize, audience, monitor, alert, management, and supply ideal answers to different safety problems that come up through the software development procedure.

In summary, the current technological environment necessitates program software safety testing as a best practice to detect vulnerabilities in the program's code, irrespective of the business's size or the business in which it functions. What is shocking, however, is that software development safety is still lagging behind and is thought of as an afterthought in many associations. Whether you would like to block your data and crucial procedures from being hacked or discontinue an internet intruder form inputting your online computer software program, alternatives to both scenarios rely on safe developed applications. That is the reason your application programmers, whether outsourced, would be the primary line of protection against dangers. It's essential that they keep a safety mindset, making sure quality assurance, testing, and code inspection.

CISSP REQUIREMENTS

In case you have planned to pick a profession in the field of data safety or if you own five or more years work experience in data security, subsequently CISSP certification will likely be the very best selection for achieving your career objective. CISSP is really called as certified information systems security professional. They're the independent kind of data security that's licensed and regulated by ISC (global information systems security certificate consortium). According to 30th June 2009, report from ISC claims that there are roughly 63,358 candidates that maintain this CISSP certification across 134 nations. CISSP was licensed American National Standard Institute (ANSI) into International Standards Organization (ISO) 17024: 2003. Thus, CISSP certification is stated as objective measures of excellence in addition to a globalized recognition benchmark.

CISSP Requirements:

1) so as to receive your CISSP credentials, then you must have knowledge and expertise in a few of these domain names.

- Risk management and information security - Access management - Cryptography - Operations safety - Regulations/ authorized / analyzes and compliance - Layout in addition to security structure - Network security and telecommunications - Disaster recovery planning and business continuity - Program security - resistant / physical safety.

2) When a candidate doesn't Have 5 years work experience, then the candidate must take a CISSP exam that's of ISC designated.

3) The ISC designated of CISSP is legal up to six years from the date of the result printed. Following that, 5 years of related work experience needs to be revealed as a way to acquire the complete CISSP status.

4) After the candidate has attained the required work experience, certification will soon be converted into CISSP certification status.

5) Attestation concerning to this professional expertise is required and the candidate must consent on this CISSP code of integrity.

6) Four criminal background backgrounds should be replied and also with related desktop.

7) Candidate must pass the CISSP examination with 700 points as a score or more.

8) Candidate must have their specialist credentials endorsed by Certified ISC at a fantastic standing. Endorser Who's demonstrating the candidate's assertion ought to be accurate and best of the knowledge.

HOW TO REGISTER

Trying to get ahead in the scientific discipline is a continuing procedure that requires dedication and diligence. After all, the competition is fierce and the ever-changing face of the technology requires a solid offence when going up the ladder of success. Among the very best or most useful approaches is to choose on CISSP certification instruction so as to boost your resume using industry-specific credentials which are recognized by companies throughout the world.

Incorporating CISSP Certification Training in your everyday schedule may not be simple when you've got a time-consuming job in addition to family or social duties. Nevertheless, the effort is well worthwhile if you would like to be successful in your chosen career path as an IT professional. Among the most flexible procedures for obtaining the CISSP Certification Training which you need is to register on to research an informative pair of CISSP Training Videos, designed to supply you with a comprehensive presentation of present CISSP subjects.

This sort of self-study training provides all the up-to-date Info you need on each subject within the world of CISSP certificate, providing you a firm foundation on which to move your career forward within the IT business.

To get the maximum from your CISSP Training Videos, then you need to create a weekly program which offers a consistent number of hours of research every week, yet lets you stay flexible on your chosen study occasions. Second, you need to attend every one of your CISSP certification coaching sessions nicely rested, entirely fed, and undistracted. Elements of your life like being hungry or tired may interfere with your learning attempts, and therefore, this may impact your ability to pass the CISSP examination. If you concentrate on every training session together with undivided attention, you will learn more quickly and economically.

Studying to become a Certified Information System Security Professional Generates a new aspect on your ability set - one which can progress your career clearly. You will improve your ability to successfully handle network infrastructure, optical coaching, coordinated wireless situations, network protection, shifting, and information storage.

Since you complete the analysis of your Entire collection of CISSP Training Videos, move ahead to your certification examination with all the assurance that you're fully ready to successfully complete the extensive range of test questions so as to acquire your CISSP certificate. Keep in mind cool and examine each question carefully to answer properly. Earn the certificate to generate a smart career, have a fantastic chance.

CISSP EXAM STRUCTURE

The CISSP Exam is considered as an instrument to measure your capacity to mitigate risk and improve safety, while doing other IT security-related activities, like managing data systems and implementing security processes. The simple fact that the CISSP is internationally recognized means successful applicants will discover ample opportunities irrespective of their location.

What's the Objective of the CISSP Exam?

The objective of The CISSP examination is to test your technical abilities, like executing and maintaining a safety program, or some other tasks which would be done by a safety auditor, systems engineer, CISO, or even safety architect.

The examination will take one to another level in your career by strengthening your abilities, fostering your self-confidence, and expanding your specialized knowledge. The CISSP is currently DoD 8759-approved and is recorded in the categories of IAT Grade III, IAM Level II, IAM Level III, IASAE I and IASAE II.

CISSP Exam Program, Duration, and Format

The CISSP Includes 250 multiple-choice that may take a few distinct kinds:

   Drag and fall --within this kind of query, you have to drag a couple of replies from 1 side of the display into a box on the opposite side of the display. Simply drag the right response (s).

Hotspot-- questions ask that you click on a particular point in a picture representation, like a diagram of community structure. The question will normally request that you identify where a specific component would be found or where a specific sort of assault is very likely to arise.

You will have three hours to finish the examination, which comprises questions from eight domain names:

· Safety and hazard management
15 percent

· Asset Safety
10 percent

· Safety architecture and technology
13 percent

· Communication and network safety
14 percent

· Identity and accessibility management
13 percent

· Safety evaluation and analyzing
12 percent

· Safety surgeries
13 percent

· Computer Software Development safety
10 percent

When to Schedule Your Assessment

Scheduling will depend entirely on your degree of preparedness for the CISSP examination. If you need time to complete as many questions as possible before taking the exam, take it.

When you're prepared, you will have to schedule your examination through the Pearson VUE site. Register to get an account, log in, and you will be presented with analyzing centre and date choices. Be aware that this information isn't available out of the Pearson VUE site, and it's only available for anyone who has a registered account.

Fixing and Taking the Assessment

To reserve the examination, follow these simple actions to be certain to satisfy each the prerequisites:

   Review the test accessibility for every examination here.
   See the Pearson VUE site.
   Create an account and examine the non-disclosure
   Select the best test centre for your place.
   Select a consultation period.
   Cover the exam.
   Maintain your confirmation email.

Once you complete the above measures, Pearson VUE will transfer your enrolment info into (ISC)2. It is also possible to register via phone; the contact numbers for Pearson VUE are available here.

Which Are the Diagnosis Requirements for Testing?

When you arrive at the testing centre, you are going to want to give staff with two valid forms of identification. The next ID choices are okay:

- A legal state-issued driver's permit
- A legal state-issued ID card
- A valid military ID
- A valid passport
- A legal green card or resident card

More Information concerning the kinds of acceptable identification with this test is available here.

What is the Exam Arrival Procedure Like?

Strategy to arrive at least 30 minutes ahead of your exam is scheduled to start. It might be a good idea to get used to the location of this exam centre; you must be prepared for other factors that may affect the trip. Arriving early could avoid any identification difficulties or questions that can be addressed without affecting the certificate effort.

You'll be photographed upon arrival and will need to leave all personal belongings beyond the testing area in a safe location. When you register, the test administrator will provide you a brief orientation and then direct you to your personal computer terminal.
Which will be the policies for rescheduling, late arrivals, and cancellations?

Online cancellations and rescheduling should be done at least 48 hours prior to the scheduled examination period. Telephone cancellations and rescheduling should be performed at least 24 hours prior to the appointment. Pearson VUE prices a rescheduling fee of $50 USD plus a cancellation charge of $100 USD. Following this stage, you should either write the examination or forfeit your enrolment fees.

Should you arrive Less than 15 minutes prior to the examination start time, you'll be considered overdue. You won't be able to write the examination and will forfeit your exam fee. Candidates will be expected to arrive at least 30 minutes prior to the examination and are set to get started. The man overseeing the examination will use her or his discretion when determining whether a candidate could write the examination after coming late. If you're turned off because of late arrival, your examination result will appear in the system for a no-show.

If You Fail the Test, When Would You Re-Take It?

If you don't pass the test on your first attempt, you'll need to wait 30 days until it is possible to re-take the exam. Should you fail another time, you'll have a 90-day waiting period until you are able to take the assessment again. Failing a third period calls for a 180-day waiting interval. You can't try this test more than three occasions in a calendar year, therefore it's essential that you're thoroughly prepared before reserving and taking the exam.

CISSP EXAM RULES

The CISSP Examination is demanding, but if you've worked your way through the frequent Body of Knowledge and know your stuff when it comes to areas like network security and disaster recovery, you ought to do good -- so long as you have read CISSP For Dummies and choose the subsequent CISSP exam test day tips to heart

· Get a fantastic night's rest. The evening before the examination is not the time to perform some other last-minute cramming. Finding a fantastic night's rest is vital.

· Dress comfortably. You ought to dress in attire that is comfortable and proper -- remember this can be a three-hour examination for specialist certification.

· Eat a fantastic meal. No matter how anxious you might be feeling, try to find something down prior to the examination. You have around 3 hours to finish the CISSP examination -- that is a very long time to go on an empty belly.

· Bring your photo ID. You want to bring your driver's permit, government-issued ID, or passport -- all these are the only types of ID that are approved.

· Bring snacks and drinks. If your testing centre allows it, think about bringing a little snack and a couple of beverages (juice, water, or soda -- beer!) to get you through the exam. Make certain that you understand the testing centre's rules and processes for shooting breaks and eating/drinking throughout the examination.

· Bring prescription or over-the-counter drugs. Again, check with your testing centre and also inform the test administrator in case you are taking any prescription medicine that has to be taken throughout the examination. Nothing can destroy your chances of success on the CISSP exam like a medical crisis! Furthermore, if you are taking any meds that are parasitic, like acetaminophen, nasal spray, or antacids to remove any annoying inconveniences like nausea, nausea, or a gastrointestinal malady, then make certain to take them until you begin the examination. A box of cells could also be appropriate -- if you've got a cold or you feel like crying when you find the exam!

· Leave your cell phone behind. Switch off your cellular phones and whatever else that moves beep or buzz.

· Take regular breaks. Three hours is a very long time. Make sure you get up and walk around throughout the examination is allowed. Otherwise, at least elongate your legs, then curl your feet, crack your knuckles, break your eyes (but do not fall asleep!), and roll up your neck -- or anything you want to do (within reason) to keep the blood flowing through the entire body. Make sure you bring a couple of short breaks throughout the examination.

Taking the True Exam

Even though the CISSP is the greatest paying certificate in Information Security, It's also among the most difficult certificates to obtain. The evaluation consists of 250 multiple choice questions answered within the length of 6-hours. 25 of those queries are "trial" questions in which the answers aren't counted towards your grade. These queries are utilized for possible inclusion at a subsequent test. The test-takers needs to pass the exam with a score of 700 or greater on a scale of 1000. The issue for test-takers is the fact that ISC2 won't disclose how they weight each query. It isn't known if some questions are weighted more than the others.

For test-takers that pass the exam, they will receive an email from ISC2 Within 6-8 months (generally more like two) letting them know they passed the evaluation. People who pass the test won't get their true score. ISC2 has stated this is to suppress any rivalry among CISSP's when incorporating credentials to matters like resumes. They prefer to state that CISSP's are equivalent. Testers that don't pass the evaluation will receive their rating and just how well they did on every one of the 10 domain names. This also aids the test-taker know what places they did badly in so that they could study them retake the examination.

ISC2 has gone to great lengths to guarantee their certificate's Credibility is shielded. They mitigate risks by ensuring access for their testing substances is strictly regulated. Test-takers need to utilize scantron sheets and ensure they turn in all materials prior to leaving the testing centre like any scratch paper which has been used. The one thing you'll be able to bring in the area with you will be a beverage and lunch. You have to continue to keep both of these in front of the area and away from your desk. Even though some proctors are a bit more lenient about the beverages. You're permitted to have a brief bathroom break, even though in the event that you're taking a very long time, the proctor might come searching for you.

So, get a Fantastic night's sleep and also Get Ready for the gruelling 6-hour test before you. Get an adequate breakfast in you as you might not have the time for lunch. Many test-takers utilize the whole 6-hours so make your body ready to take as few breaks as possible. Get there early and go over your notes one final time before going into the classroom. Read each question carefully and don't rush choosing the "best" response. A good deal of the queries may have multiple answers which are right, however, you'll want to determine the "best" response.

CISSP 8 DOMAINS

The CISSP® (Accredited Info Systems Security Professional) eligibility is among the most respected certifications in the information security business, demonstrating an innovative understanding of cyber protection.

We lately discussed the advantages of being a CISSP. We turn our focus on the construction of this qualification itself as well as also the domain names inside.

(ISC)2, which Developed and keeps the CISSP eligibility, updated the arrangement of this certification in 2015, moving out of ten domain names.

We'll start by listing the eight domain names, then proceed on to describe each one in more detail.
Which will be the 8 CISSP domain names?

- Safety and Risk Control
- Asset Security
- Safety Architecture and Engineering
- Communications and Network Security
- Identity and Access Control
- Safety Assessment and Testing
- Security Operations
- Software Development Security

1) Safety and Risk Control

Safety and Risk Management includes about 15 percent of the CISSP examination.

This is the biggest domain names in CISSP, offering an extensive breakdown of the situations you want to learn about information systems management. It covers:

The confidentiality, integrity, and availability of data;
- Safety Management principles;
- Compliance demands;
- regulatory and legal issues about data security;
- IT policies and processes; and
- Risk-based management theories.

2) Asset Security

Asset Security includes about 10 percent of the CISSP examination.

This domain name Addresses the physical essentials of information protection. It covers:

The classification and possession of assets and information;
- Privacy;
- Retention intervals;
- Data safety controllers; and handling demands.

3) Security Architecture and Engineering

Safety Engineering includes about 13 percent of the CISSP exam.

This domain name Covers several significant data security concepts, such as:

- Engineering procedures utilizing secure design fundamentals;
- Fundamental theories of safety versions;

- Safety capacities of data technologies;
- Assessing and mitigating vulnerabilities in programs;
- Cryptography; and
- Designing and implementing physical safety.

4) Communications and Network Security

Communications and Network Security includes about 14 percent of the CISSP examination.

This domain name Covers the protection and design of the organization's systems. Including:

- Safe layout principles for community design;
- Safe network elements; and
- Secure communication stations.

5) Identity and Access Control

Identity and Access Management includes about 13 percent of the CISSP examination.

This domain name Helps data security professionals know how to control how users can get info. It covers:

- Physical and logical access to resources;
- Identification and authentication;
- Integrating identity for service and third-party identity solutions;
- Authorization mechanics; and
- The identification and access provisioning lifecycle.

6) Security Assessment and Testing

Safety Assessment and Testing include about 12 percent of the CISSP examination.

This domain name Focuses on the design, performance, and evaluation of safety testing. It includes:

- Designing and validating assessment and evaluation plans;
- Safety control testing;
- Collecting security procedure information;
- Exam Cards;
- Internal and third-party safety audits.

7) Security Operations

Safety Operations includes about 13 percent of the CISSP examination.

This domain name Addresses how plans are put into action. It covers:

- Recognizing and encouraging investigations;
- Prerequisites for evaluation types;
- Logging and tracking actions;
- Securing the supply of tools;
- Foundational security operations notions;
- Implementing resource security methods;
- Incident direction;
- Disaster recovery;
- Handling physical safety; and
- Business continuity.

8) Software Development Security

Software Development Security includes about 10 percent of the CISSP exam.

This domain name Helps professionals to comprehend, apply and enforce software safety. It covers:

- Safety in the applications development life cycle;
- Safety controls in growth environments;
- Efficacy of applications safety; and
- Safe coding guidelines and criteria.

HOW TO PLAN YOUR STUDY FOR CISSP

Making the Perfect (ISC)2 CISSP Study Plan

Safety. It is in everybody's mind. CTO Magazine rated safety as the #1 problem facing CIOs today. That means that safety represents a fantastic career opportunity for experienced IT professionals searching for a shift.

The Certified Information Systems Security Professional (CISSP) in the International Information System Security Certification Consortium, or (ISC)², is considered one of the most precious -- and roughest -- safety certificates.

In their Present Guide to the CISSP, (ISC)² asserts that CISSP-certified professionals earn an average salary of over $130,000. The Cyberese interactive cyber-security supply/demand map of project postings revealed the CISSP has been the most asked security certificate.

Getting the CISSP Certificate isn't a walk through the playground. That is why we've laid out a research plan that will help you become prepared on test day.

Move with Caution

CISSP Isn't For novices. If you're trying to find a means to kick-start your cyber-security profession, the Systems Security Certified Practitioner (SSCP) from (ISC)2 and CompTIA's Security+ are equally fantastic vendor-neutral entry-level certificates. Both are also U.S. Department of Défense (DOD) Directive 8570.1 baseline certs for Level II Information Assurance Tech (IAT) jobs. SSCP is approved for Level I tasks.

CISSP, on the other hand, is a certificate for experienced security specialists. In most large businesses, the CISSP certificate is needed for career development. For your U.S. government, it is a baseline cert for Level III IA Technician tasks -- and for tasks in Level II or III Information Assurance Manager (IAM) and Level I and II IA System Architects and Engineers (IASAE).

The CISSP Covers eight domain names from Risk and Security Control to Software Development Security. To be certified as a CISSP, then you have to pass the CISSP examination AND have recorded five years of paid, full-time occupation in a few of those domain names. You will find other strategies to count CISSP expertise, but you still require serious safety work experience under your belt to be eligible.

As mentioned before, the examination covers the eight domains of safety together with the following weightings:

- Safety and Risk Management: 15 percent
- Asset Security: 10 percent
- Safety Architecture and Engineering: 13 percent
- Communication and Network Security: 14 percent
- Identity and Access Management (IAM): 13 percent
- Safety Assessment and Testing: 12 percent
- Safety Operations: 13 percent

- Software Development Security: 10 percent

Utilizing CBT Nuggets for CISSP Accredited

CBT Nuggets Supplies a complete selection of instruction to help prepare one for CISSP certification. Actually, Keith Barker and Ben Finkel -- among our specialist coaches -- worked together to make a video-training playlist for CISSP certification. This playlist comprises eight abilities covering the eight domain names connected with the examination. Overall, it provides up to 95 CBT Nuggets movies and nine hours of instruction.

To help reinforce and confirm your learning, every ability includes both in-video and post-video quiz questions. Have a look at our latest blog article introducing Keith and Ben's (ISC)2 CISSP 2018 coaching and observe a totally free Nugget on the best way best to resolve identity management (IDM).

Your Own CISSP Study Plan

So, you've decided to pull the trigger and also examine for your CISSP certification? You will find nine hours of CBT Nuggets CISSP training. It is possible to observe an hour of movies per week and undergo our whole training in fourteen days. But there is much more to learning than simply watching movies. You understand better if you fortify your comprehension through practical laboratory exercises and examine your retention together with practice examinations.

Everyone Learns in their own manner, which means that your CISSP study travel has to be personalized to your specific needs. To begin, we have assembled a

9-week CISSP certification study program. It leans heavily on CBT Nuggets CISSP coaching, together with practice examinations and additional tools. In building this program, we planned to comprise about one hour of video instruction each week -- more or not.

How Long Should You Read?

CBT Nuggets Training shouldn't be your sole resource to prepare for the CISSP. This is a challenging exam. It isn't a technical examination. It is a management test. Such as the PMP or ITIL, the CISSP supports whether you're able to look at safety problems through the lens of (ISC)two methodologies. Fourteen days is a great beginning point, but you will probably want more time. How much time? That is determined by what you already understand, and how much time you have been at work.

Let us get started.

Week 1: Assess Your Awareness

Require a practice examination. It is very good to establish in the get-go what you do and do not understand. Thus, your first step must be to choose a practice examination. You may either purchase the Official (ISC)² CISSP Practice Tests novel or utilize the Kaplan® IT Training clinic examinations which are included using a CBT Nuggets subscription. Whichever course you choose, your clinic examination results can allow you to set a knowledge baseline.

Together with your Practice examination completed, you need to begin on the Information Security: Security and Risk Management ability. View Nuggets videos through 11. In these modules, CBT Nuggets coach Keith Barker presents the philosophical theories of safety and threat management, such as:

    Confidentiality, integrity, and accessibility
    Safety governance and compliance
    Establishing and maintaining security knowledge and education
    Identifying business continuity requirements.

After every video, reinforce your understanding by answering the custom questions to the modules in the (ISC)two or Kaplan® IT Training clinic examinations. The latter, of that again, is comprised using a CBT Nuggets subscription.

Weekly time commitment: 4 hours. The Kaplan® IT Training clinic exam must take you about fourteen days. The 11 movie Nuggets are 50 minutes long.

Week 2: Security and Risk Management & Asset Security

Begin that week by viewing the last four movie Nuggets in the Information Security: Security and Risk Management skill. They ensure intellectual property and licensing, hazard modelling, supply chain risk management, and coverage lifecycle.

Next, see the Information Safety: Asset Security ability. Keith covers the Essential issues of asset safety, Including privacy protection, strength retention, and data protection controls.
Weekly time commitment: 1 hour. The Asset Security ability comprises seven movies to get a total of 35 minutes. Together with the four Safety and Risk

Control videos, week two's instruction must require 58 minutes.

Week 3: Security Architecture

When you've obtained the asset security ability under your belt, see the initial 12 Nuggets of all information security: Security Architecture and Engineering. You'll be delving in the following abilities in those videos:

- Designing with safety in mind
- The variety of security models and their intentions
- Prerequisites for system safety
- Safety capacities of hardware and firmware
- Safety vulnerabilities and how to evaluate them in online systems, cellular platforms, and embedded devices
- Symmetric and asymmetric keys and encryption.

Weekly time commitment: 1 hour. These 12 movie Nuggets include a totalled 62 moments.

Week 4: Security Architecture & Network Security

This week, you will round from the Information Security: Security Architecture and Engineering ability by viewing videos 13 through 17. You are going to find out how to mitigate vulnerabilities in online systems, cellular systems, and embedded devices. You will also learn how to use cryptography.

When you're satisfied that you have mastered these issues, proceed into the Information Security:

Communication and Network Security ability. You will get a comprehension of these themes:

- Safe layout fundamentals in community architectures
- Network elements, including Network Access Control (NAC)
- Secure communication channels, for example, remote access.

Weekly time commitment: 1 hour. The Communication and Network Security ability includes six movies that complete 38 minutes. Together with the five Security Architecture and Engineering videos, the Week 4 movies are going to take a total of 59 minutes.

Week 5: IAM (and Test Your Knowledge)

You are currently at the midway stage of the CISSP security domain. It is time to choose your next practice exam. Even though you may only test on the initial four domain names, we advise that you take the whole examination. You're going to find a clearer idea of just how well you are learning all of the content. The examination results will even help you figure out which domains may require a bit more focus on another time around.

Okay, mock examination finished? You did better than you ever anticipated? Great. Let us proceed to Information Security: Identity and Access Management (IAM) skill. Keith can enable you to understand identity and access management (IAM) while covering these abilities:

- Physical and logical access to resources

- Identification and authentication of individuals, apparatus, and services
- Authorization mechanics, including role-based access control (RBAC) and mandatory access control (MAC).

Weekly time commitment: 4 hours. The nine IAM movie Nuggets complete 50 minutes. If you tack on a different full-size practice examination, add three hours for this week's studies.

Week 6: Security Assessment and Operations

This week has you completing the Information Security: Security Assessment and Testing ability. You are also likely to take your initial bite from Information Security: Security Operations skill.

The Safety Assessment and Testing ability are rather short -- six movie Nuggets totalling 29 minutes. Key topics you will discover include vulnerability assessments, penetration testing, log reviews, and safety instructions.

The Safety Operations ability is 27 videos extended and will take two or more hours. Because of this, we have spread it over three months. This week, you are going to observe the first nine movies covering that ability.

You will develop a comprehension of safety operations, while studying the elements of investigations, such as evidence collection and electronic forensics tools. You will also receive a brief introduction to executing disaster recovery and business continuity programs.

Weekly Time commitment: Slightly over 1 hour. The Security Assessment and Testing movies together with the initial nine Security Operations Nuggets means Week 6 videos will require approximately 68 minutes to see.

Week 7: More Security Operations

This week, you need to continue with Information Security: Security Operations, watching Nuggets 10 through 22. You will continue to develop your comprehension of security operations while studying about the next:

- Incident response and managing
- Patch and alter the direction
- Intrusion detection and intrusion prevention
- Firewalls
- Vulnerability scoring.

Weekly time commitment: 1 hour. All these 13 Nuggets complete 62 minutes.

Week 8: More Security Operations

This week, you will complete Information Security: Security Operations ability, viewing videos 23 -- 27. You will develop a comprehension of security operations, especially cantered on business continuity (BC) and disaster recovery (DR). These modules cover the following:

- Fault tolerance for accessibility
- Disaster recovery and alternative sites
- equipment and applications preparation for DR
- DR communications and management

- Personal security and safety in the event of a BCDR occasion

As soon as you're satisfied that you know these topics, proceed to the last CISSP domain -- Software Development Security. Additionally, this is where Keith hands-on teaching duties to Ben Finkel, our application development specialist.

During the Information Security: Software Development Security ability, Ben can help you comprehend of applications development safety while covering subjects such as procuring the applications development life cycle (SDLC), analyzing the safety impact of acquired applications, and implementing programming criteria.

Weekly Time commitment: Slightly over 1 hour. The closing Security Operations videos, together with the eight Software Development Security videos may require 72 minutes. It is slightly more than an hour week. However, take a glimpse, your closing week of research is complete!

Week 9: You are Finished with CBT Nuggets Training!

After completion of all the CBT Nuggets CISSP abilities, it is time for one more practice examination. At this time, you'll have the ability to completely evaluate what you've heard -- and also identify additional inspection areas before you sit for the official exam. Make sure you return to individual videos as required to reinforce or review your own knowledge.

Weekly time commitment: 3 hours (at least). To sit another full-size clinic exam and give yourself at least three to four hours.

Week 10+: What is Next?

You can easily complete CBT Nuggets training in 9 weeks, but do not stop there. The CISSP is a challenging examination with notoriously hard questions. Keep reading until you are constantly passing CISSP practice exams and feel comfy with all the minutiae of the (ISC)2 modalities.

Can Be CISSP for You?

CISSP Certificate might not be perfect for you. There are additional security certification choices that may serve you better, determined by your function, your company, or your own career ambitions.

IT Security Certifications: The Breakdown has helpful facts about the array of vendor-neutral security certificates that are available -- such as CISSP.

If you are attempting to determine whether the CISSP certificate is logical for you, you also need to examine the (ISC)² Ultimate Guide to the CISSP. This will supply you with additional details about the actions to -- and advantages of -- getting a CISSP.

For additional advice about the CISSP exam itself, download the CISSP Exam Review and examine in detail the test topics covered under each of the safety domains.

30 DAYS STUDY PLAN

This examination prep manual contains four stages: strategy, review, practice, evaluation. In the subsequent sections, I will offer a brief summary of what is done in every stage. This manual is aimed primarily at experienced IT professionals. Lots of you may easily have the ability to finish this certificate in 30 days (or less) by following this program.

Days 0 to 2: Planning Stage

The objective of this stage is to be sure to create a research program that Addresses all of the CISSP material. Too many men and women bypass this step and are amazed to learn that they did not spend enough time researching what is really on the evaluation. There's not any explanation for this. (ISC)2 tells you upfront what is likely to be about the exam!

Tasks:

- Inspection of the CISSP CIB (aka Certification Assessment Review).
- Program the examination.
- Produce your research plan (or follow this one).

Recommendations:
Produce a dedicated record or laptop to your CISSP studies. I use OneNote, however, there are scores of great options, including paper laptops.
Publish a copy of the CIB or write down the goals on your laptop.
Schedule your test Straight Away! The very best time I'd suggest to invest in the examination is fourteen days. 1 week for each domain, and another for

inspection. Should you follow this guide, you should not need over 30 days.

Set aside a regular study period. If you're able to devote 90 minutes every day during the next 30 days to make it through this process, daily 30 you will have spent 45 hours of research time preparing for the CISSP.

Days 2 to 10: Review Stage

The objective of this stage is to be certain to truly cover all of the appropriate test substance. Do not waste too much time at this stage. Your goal here is to find a high-profile overview of what is on the examination. Do not be worried if you do not know the CISSP topics straight away. You will do a deeper dive into the substance at another stage.

Tasks:

Identify and examine the very useful exam preparation material.

Recommendations:

Select two to three main references to find out from. No more. I Suggest Eric Conrad's Eleventh Hour CISSP, his CISSP Study Guide, along with also the CISSP Course by Cybrary.it. The Sybex CISSP Study Guide by James Stewart along with also the CISSP All-in-One by Shon Harris will also be popular.

Listen to sound videos or courses in 1.5x to 2x speed to get through the content quicker.

Usage The Pareto Principle (20 percent of composed material conveys 80 percent of the data) to lessen your reading period:

Browse the front and back book covers, table of contents, intro, and decision to comprehend how the book is organized.

Read through the glossary and index. Highlight and examine any terms which are unfamiliar to you.

Skim the rest of the publication. Be conscious of bold or italicized notes, words, tables, and charts.

Instantly review every chapter. Read the first few paragraphs of each paragraph to understand the writer's key points for every segment. Review the chapter outline and any review queries.

When the chapter does not have an inventory, then outline the chapter in your own words.

Days 10 to 25: Practice Stage

The clinic stage is where the majority of your actual learning occurs, therefore it needs to be the stage in which you spend the majority of your time. You need to expect it to require one or two weeks to make it through this stage.

For knowledge-based tests such as the CISSP, I suggest practicing for the examination using the Feynman Technique. Using the Feynman Technique, you examine your knowledge of the content by instructing (or faking to instruct) it to other people. The Feynman Technique takes four steps:

Take out your examination prep laptop and write one subject in the CIB at the peak of each webpage.

Write down as much info as you can about the subject. Force yourself to use straightforward terms. Pretend as if you are instructing it to a course.

If you get stuck on a subject, return to the source material to acquire a better knowledge of it.

Simplify further and use analogies to explain the substance.

Using the Feynman Technique is your single-best approach to ensure a pass to the CISSP examination. It is a far better use of the time compared to re-reading the substance or moving over unfinished study notes.

Tasks

Utilize the Feynman Technique to educate yourself challenging CISSP topics.

Recommendations:

Reference more comprehensive substance as required to fill in knowledge gaps. You're able to use more thorough CISSP study guides (like the Shon Harris novels) or the supplemental references in the CIB.
After inputting your notes, use the Hemingway Editor App to examine how clear that your writing is. Shoot to your 8th-grade lower or level.
Scott Young has a Terrific four-minute intro into the Feynman Technique here: https://www.youtube.com/watch?v=FrNqSLPaZLc

Days 25 to 30: Test Stage

From the week Leading to the examination, you ought to take a minimum of one practice test that simulates the terms of the actual examination. Transcender.com along with also the CCCure Quiz Engine provide practice tests that you could utilize to prepare one for the actual examination. Practice tests are helpful for assisting you to identify gaps in your own learning.

Should you miss any queries on the practice examination, return and review the appropriate material using the Feynman technique.

In terms of the actual evaluation: there are dozens of suggestions online about how to make it through the examination. In my experience, it boils down to relaxation and preparation.

There is nothing particular about the evaluation day. Simply show up and take the exam.

If you have followed all of the steps up to the stage, passing the evaluation is merely a natural effect of all of the hard work you install. Get a fantastic night's rest, eat a fantastic meal, and be sure that you appear on time and prepared to take the exam. The rest is simply a formality.

Tasks:

   Take a training test on day 25 (or sooner) to spot any gaps in your own learning.
   Utilize the Feynman Technique to return over any substance that you are unsure about.
   On test day, show up on time and get prepared to take the real exam.

Recommendations:

   Take a while to read up on test-day hints from some other writers. I discovered Cyber-security Test Tips and Techniques by Jim West for a Fantastic resource.
   Do not allow the horror stories to dissuade you: I discovered the CISSP examination to become much easier than many individuals claim. It is nowhere near

as tough as the CISSP concentration tests or the CISM. But if you've never accepted a certification test before, it may be challenging. Do not take it too softly.

Planning and comfort will be the keys to achievement. If you have completed the correct quantity of prep work (40+ hours of research), then the real examination is simple. Knowing that the evaluation is simple can help you unwind while moving through it.

WHY YOU NEED TO JOIN A STUDY GROUP

So, you have just started to research for the CISSP examination, you immediately Realized it is a really big challenge on your own and you've opted to split the issue into small chunks and form a study group in your region. This really is a really good initiative on your part, I firmly urge such a research group. But I must warn you that it isn't necessarily simple and it needs to be sustained with a committed group of volunteers. Below you'll see some suggestions about the best way best to start, things to do as soon as you've begun the class, and a couple of suggestions on the examination prep too.

FORMING YOUR VERY OWN STUDY GROUP

1. PUBLICIZE YOUR INITIATIVE. The initial step is to market your initiative, under you've got a couple excellent places to get started.

2. START SMALL and EXPAND. Collect a bunch of people together who are ready to engage and aid in preparing the research team. Don't wait till you've got an extremely large number, it's much better to conduct a small workshop in the start to iron the bugs out and also to acquire improved contacts. A tiny group of interested individuals is far better than a bunch that doesn't want to actively take part but just benefits from the bunch. What I typically predict leeches. We do not need leeches, all members need to do their part to the team to work.

3. BE A FACILITATOR, NOT AN EXPERT. Search for volunteers with enough energy and time to ease a domain a guide, a part of a domain name, provided everything else going on in their own personal, family, and work lives. Request facilitators. Do not expect people to become experts on this issue. The facilitator prepares by studying the content enough to determine puzzling stuff or primary points for debate. The facilitator's aim is to make it much easier for folks to comprehend the topic or subject enough therefore that the material is more inclined to make feel as individuals study the frequent body of knowledge in the future. Do not ask facilitators to prepare extended presentations or heaps of queries. The harder and time-intensive it is, the fewer people will volunteer. The facilitator may want to only use a yellow highlighter for keywords or concepts which need to be discussed. Encourage individuals to share important personal stories and expert knowledge as you talk as a team. Frequently time real-life case will induce the stage and you will not forget about it.

4. BE FLEXIBLE IN YOUR APPROACH Don't expect anything, kindly ask and hope for the better. Participants will be different. Accept that people aren't able to come to each meeting. Occasionally everyone needs time to get private interests, family members, or work at precisely the exact same time as the research group meeting. Our team size varies from three to about seven distinct individuals each week.

5. FREQUENCY OF MEETING you need to choose the frequency and times which you want to conduct your coaching sessions. You need to consider how long the coaching session will function as well. I'd say: Don't meet more frequently than once every week, you will need the time to digest new stuff and to think of new

stuff from meeting to meeting. As a general principle: meet as frequently as realistic on a standard schedule. Meet in a time that's suitable for most people. I've observed research groups that match on Saturdays from 1-3 pm although some are going to meet at night throughout the week. Most study groups don't meet on holiday vacations or on weekends. Don't attempt and schedule a meeting at the centre of the vacation season. Groups will usually cease within the vacation or vacation season and resume once the new year begins.

6. MUTUAL RESPECT Mutual Respect is of extreme importance. Most of us have our weaknesses and strength and also our great day and a bad day. As my buddy Ginger advocated: Treat everyone with respect. We welcome anybody mad enough to decide to commit their time in sharing, playing, and studying with us in our meetings. Folks are invited to come back even if they don't have enough time to read the content prior to the assembly. Individuals are treated with regard to their intellect however little or much they know about every one of the safety domains. The concept will be to help each other know the safety domain names, share adventures, inspire each other, and demonstrate our understanding from passing the CISSP examination.

7. Select a TARGET DATE FOR THE EXAM as soon as you've got a big enough group, you need to set up a target date which you want to take the examination. I'd say you ought to begin studying approximately 3 to 4 weeks before the examination so as to properly prepare. As soon as you've picked a date, then you have to use that data to construct your group study program.

8. SELECT AN APPROPRIATE LOCATION Today you need to make sure you have somewhere to satisfy that's big enough for your group and that's readily available for everybody. Among the major factor of success are location, location, and place. Meet in precisely the exact same place as far as you can. Folks are unwilling to discover that they're in the incorrect location. Always include clear instructions to the meeting place on your announcement emails which are most likely to be offered to other interested men and women. The instructions make it effortless for all these new folks to locate you. A map like Google Maps could be transmitted to the attendees in advance. Possessing a place near public transport could help also. Assign an individual which will be in charge of welcome people in the assembly. It may indicate that this individual will open and shut the centre for each study team meeting. It's always good to have a person come early to post signs about the construction and office suite doorways if it's required. The safety guard may not be conscious of the assembly, let him understand it's running and in which area it's being conducted, he'll then have the ability to direct people to the appropriate site.

9. Use YOUR GROUP EXPERTISE consider the experience you have one of the manhood of the study team and have them educate the components they are comfortable or even specialist in the slightest. For instance Clement can instruct Network safety at the very first meeting, somebody else educates Cryptography the next week, etc.

10. SEEK HELP IF NEEDED If desired get specialists from outside companies to come and teach certain topics. It gives credibility to the company that can come to instruct and also you get top-notch training.

It's a Win-Win circumstance. Obviously, you'll require somebody that organizes such instruction, it doesn't occur alone.

11. KNOW THY PEOPLE At the very first meeting, make sure that you go round the table and permit folks to present themselves so people know each other and it is also possible to find out who's great in particular places. This will also aid in breaking up the ice to the very first assembly.

12. ESTABLISH COMMUNICATION Establish communication between the associates. This is a really important point. You can use my CISSP mailing list should you desire. In this manner, you currently have a bunch of folks who are able to start training and assisting your members.

13. SHARE YOUR GROUP EXPERIENCE WITH THE COMMUNITY make sure that you discuss your expertise, achievement, issues with the neighbourhood so they can boost their research group too.

14. CRAM SESSION AND QUIZZES once a while coordinated CRAM sessions where you are able to go through queries. Invite individuals to try out the online quiz at https://cccure.education whilst taking practice tests to make sure that you observe these queries that you missed or which you had trouble. In the following meeting, you can discuss these concerns with your co-workers.

15. DO NOT REINVENT THE WHEEL Utilize the tools which are available, don't reinvent the wheel.

CISSP TRAINING SEMINARS

Certified Information Systems Security Professional (CISSP) is an Independent data security certificate governed by then on-International Information Systems Security Certification Consortium, (ISC)2.

The CISSP certification was the very first credential in the field of Information safety, licensed by the ANSI (American National Standards Institute) into ISO (International Standards Organization) Standard 17024:2003. It's accepted by the U.S. Department of Defense (DoD) in both the Information Assurance Technical (IAT) and Managerial (IAM) categories. CISSP certified professionals are considered government on key safety issues such as mobile safety, hazard management, program development protection, cloud computing systems, amongst others.

CISSP certification Isn't only an objective measure of excellence, but a globally recognized standard of achievement for safety training. Koenig provides detailed CISSP training for participants who want to obtain experience in defining the layout, structure, controls, and management resulting in a protected business environment. Individuals owning this seller neutral credential are high in demand by companies all around the world that wish to safeguard their organizations from a growth spurt of cyber-attacks.

Who must do a CISSP Course?

CISSP training is Perfect for the following professionals:

- Chief Information Security Officers (CISO)
- IT Directors
- IT Security Consultants/Managers
- Safety Architects/Auditors
- IT Managers
- Security System Engineers
- Network Architects
- CISSP Program Aims

Know the fundamentals of network and telecommunication security concepts, necessary components for reducing safety risks, securing channels of communication, and methods for preventing and discovering network-based strikes.

Describe the important terms and procedures of safety operations and the way to safeguard and control data processing resources in a centralized or distributed environment within this CISSP training.

Define and employ information security governance and Risk Control Framework including regulations, theories, principles, structures and criteria that are created for the security of data assets and how to assess the effectiveness of the protection

Profit the necessary skills to design the structure and handle IT security in a business environment via this approved CISSP class

WHERE TO STUDY AND WHY IT'S IMPORTANT TO USE MULTIPLE SOURCES

Stage 1: Deciding To Choose the Certification:

It's very important for You to Have a clean head and doubtlessly Finalization would be asked to have a need for obtaining this certificate in the brain of their candidates. Before gaining it's necessary that you check each of the advantages and disadvantages of the certificate and assess it whether it's the one that you desire. Do not just follow somebody who accomplishes any certificate, with no appropriate understanding of a specific certificate, simply because he or she states or even the whole world asks you to do so. Alternatively, you'd be necessary to look over your work, your own strengths, weaknesses and above all the true region of interest within the specialty.

Personally, I have cleared the SSCP examination provided by ISC2 in approximately 2014 and therefore CISSP would be regarded as the next development for me. I've been working within the business of data security for the previous five years since I have enquired and have understood this to acquire the CISSP certification, one wants to possess experience of five years in a couple of the domain names of CISSP CBK.

As soon as you have clearly chosen to acquire the CISSP certification, it would allow you a whole lot to become more focused on your research as you'll have the ability to study better having an open mind than having difficulty of deciding on the certificate programs.it is quite important to be concentrated in your own study.

Stage 2: Organizing

There are multiple methods to choose for the preparation of this examination; There are lots of books out there for the preparation of this examination. No matter the publication you decide to study, you're essential to pick the 1 book which is for you personally, your principal source of analyzing. The most significant thing which you have to place your focus on throughout the groundwork will make your theories clear. You're not only assumed to learn several definitions, but you'd also have to know the principles of the idea. You're necessary to keep in mind you won't be analyzed in your cramming skills within this particular exam. The examination is organized in such a way that you would not just bring out your fundamentals and clear all of the notions which will come to your rescue to get a perplexing question.

There are lots of IT professionals that wish to pass the CISSP examination effortlessly but it isn't quite as simple as you might believe. CISSP is a certification that produces a strong effect on your portfolio if you'd like success in CISSP examination then proceed with an internet resource which provides you confirmed questions and responses for CISSP examination but there are lots of internet programs that aren't giving true CISSP questions together with verified answers and which is going to be the reason many IT professionals collapsed in their closing CISSP examination.

As you understand the CISSP examination is among the most challenging examinations in the IT industry. CISSP examination demands lots of CISSP prep inquiries and also confirmed the CISSP study substance to make a fantastic passing score from the CISSP examination. DumpsBuzz established a group of highly competent professionals on this topic to make the very best CISSP exam dumps for their clientele. CISSP training stuff they supply for the CISSP examination is the best that you can discover online.

So you need to choose an internet platform that provides you the very best study material for the CISSP examination. If you readily found it then I'm certain that you Will get great grades in the only first effort. Since I passed my CISSP closing exam a couple of months back and the rationale for my success is merely an internet supply which provides me confirmed CISSP dumps that is why I'm saying a fantastic online supply will create the powerful effect on your CISSP final outcome. If you would like to understand from where I passed the CISSP examination then its title is Dumps buzz I just need to tell you they're good in what they're providing to their customers.

If you want to pass the CISSP exam with good grades, and looking for the latest CISSP dumps to prepare for the CISSP examination is only the first attempt then Dumps buzz will be the best option for you to achieve superior grades in CISSP exam. Their direction ready these latest CISSP prep questions and answers to make certain you can 100% pass CISSP examination in the just first effort easily.

They're a user-driven online platform in IT examinations. Their hired professionals who passed their CISSP exam, well contribute to creating CISSP exam dumps upgraded with CISSP new questions. To ensure you clean your CISSP certification exam initially effort.

Upgraded ISC2 CISSP Questions & Answers

Splendid contribution from their licensed pros and CISSP Experts enables us to provide the most updated and appropriate CISSP practice questions which make a fantastic impact on my final result in the CISSP exam.

CISSP Exam Practice Test Questions

Their online CISSP exam questions were created to educate their candidates about the skills needed to pass the CISSP exam.

HOW TO PRACTICE WITH PAST QUESTIONS AND WHERE TO FIND THEM

The objective of the sample question set is to supply you with information concerning the ISC2 Information Systems Security Professional (CISSP) exam. These sample questions will make you very familiar with the kind and the difficulty level of the questions on the CISSP certification test. To get familiar with the real exam environment, we suggest you try our Sample ISC2 CISSP Certification Practice Assessment. This sample practice exam gives you the sensation of fact and is an idea to the questions asked in the actual ISC2 Certified Information Systems Security Professional (CISSP) certification exam.

These sample queries are simple and fundamental questions that Represent likeness to the real ISC2 Information Systems Security Professional exam questions. To assess your readiness and functionality with real-time scenario-based questions, we suggest you prepare together with our Premium ISC2 CISSP Certification Practice Exam. When you resolve real-time scenario-based queries almost, you come across many issues that provide you an opportunity to improve.
ISC2 CISSP Sample Questions:

01. The procedure for developing an ISCM plan and implementing an ISCM software is?

A) Define, analyze, execute, establish, Respond, review and update

B) Assess, implement, define, establish, Respond, review and upgrade

C) Define, establish, implement, analyze, Respond, review and update

D) Implement, define, establish, analyze, react, Review and upgrade

02. Which are the seven primary Types of access control?

A) Detective, corrective, monitoring, logging, Recovery, classification, and directive

B) Directive, deterrent, preventative, Detective, corrective, compensating, and retrieval

C) Authorization, identification, variable, corrective, privilege, detective, and directive

D) Identification, authentication, Authorization, detective, corrective, retrieval, and directive

03. Ann installs a brand-new Wireless Access Point (WAP) and consumers can connect to it. However, once connected, users can't access the net. Which of these is the MOST likely cause of the problem?

A) The signal strength has been degraded and latency is increasing hop count.

B) An incorrect subnet mask has been entered into the WAP configuration.

C) The signal power has been degraded and packets are being lost.

D) Consumers have specified the wrong encryption type and packets are being refused.

04. Qualitative risk assessment is earmarked through the following?

A) Ease of implementation and it can be completed by personnel with limited comprehension of the risk assessment procedure

B) Can be completed by personnel with a restricted understanding of the hazard assessment procedure and utilizes detailed metrics used for calculation of danger

C) Detailed metrics used for calculation of risk and ease of execution

D) Can be completed by employees with a restricted understanding of the risk assessment procedure and detailed metrics used for the calculation of danger

05. Which of the following security models is mostly concerned with how the topics and objects are made and the way that topics are assigned rights or privileges?

A) Bell--LaPadula

B) Biba-Integrity

C) Chinese Wall

D) Graham--Denning

06. Before employing a Program Update to manufacturing systems, it is MOST important that

A) Complete disclosure information about the danger that the patch Addresses is available

B) The patching procedure is documented

C) The production systems are supported up

D) An independent third party attests the validity of this patch

07. While an Enterprise Security Architecture (ESA) can be applied in many different ways, it is focused on a few important goals. Identify the proper record of those aims for your ESA:

A) It represents a simple, long term perspective of controller, it gives a unified vision for shared security controls, it leverages existing technology investments, it supplies a fixed approach to current and future dangers and also the needs of peripheral capabilities

B) It signifies a simple, long term perspective of control, it provides a unified vision for shared security controls, it leverages new technology investments, it provides a flexible approach to current and future dangers as well as the needs of core functions

C) It represents a complicated, short term perspective of controller, it provides a unified vision for shared security controls, and it leverages existing technology investments, it provides a flexible way of current and future dangers as well as the needs of core functions

D) It represents a simple, long term view of controller, it gives a unified vision for shared security controls, so it leverages existing technology investments, it provides a flexible way of current and future threats as well as the requirements of core functions

08. Technical evaluation of assurance to make certain that security requirements have been met is known as?

A) Certification

B) Certification

C) Validation

D) Verification

09. A potential vulnerability of the kerberos authentication server is

A) Single point of failure

B) Asymmetric key compromise

C) Use of dynamic passwords

D) Limited lifetimes for authentication credentials

10. Which of these can BEST be used to capture comprehensive security requirements?

A) Threat modelling, covert channels, and information classification

B) Info classification, hazard assessments, and covert channels

C) Risk evaluations, covert channels, and danger modelling

D) Threat modelling, data classification, and risk assessments

Answers:

Question: 01 Response: c

Question: 02 Response: b

Query: 03 Response: b

Query: 04 Response: a

Query: 05 Answer: d

Question: 06 Answer: c

Question: 07 Response: d

Query: 08 Answer: b

Query: 09 Response: a

Query: 10 Answer: d

HOW TO MANAGE YOUR TIME DURING EXAMS

Not wishing to cause alarm however, the CISSP examination is six hours long and contains a total of 250 multiple-choice questions. It's an exercise not only for your mind and thoughtful risk management but also in endurance and endurance during its full capacity.
A good night's sleep and a couple of chocolates!

It's important for you to get a good night's sleep prior to your exam (hopefully!) to make sure your concentration levels are at their best. A useful exam day tip: take a couple of snacks (energy boosters), a calculator and an English dictionary (if you're writing your examination in English) together with you. The dictionary and calculator are usually allowed within the exam hall and might be of help to you but before you set them in your luggage, check the most recent exam rules on the ISC2 website under 'Exam Policies and Procedures'.

It belongs without saying that if sitting your exam, commit to giving your best, whatever occurs. There's a general guideline in that you have to believe the way a risk management consultant with logic; significance how the problem stated in the question would have been approached from senior management (policy/procedures) to centre management (project management), and to technology (alternative execution).

Take a Rest and stretch

It is recommended that you take three breaks within the six-hour time interval, preferably in a logical order but there's not any rule to if you take your own breaks. Plan them if it suits you, i.e. at two-hourly intervals, or any time you believe that your mind (and muscles!) Need a break and some fresh air. A good way of increasing the intake of oxygen to help concentrate is to take some deep breaths and stretch those muscles on your breaks.

A circle of queries

The CISSP examination is computer-based which lets you navigate freely between the queries. It is advised that the examination is approached in a round way; i.e. consider all of the questions as though they're in a big circle. So, in the first circle, aim the questions that have a brief "question announcement" or appear to be difficult and wouldn't take you over two minutes to finish at the first attempt. This approach will help to boost your confidence as you progress around the circle of queries, completing all the easier-to-score questions, which could amount to approximately 100!

An the same time you're targeting the easier questions, mark other queries of more difficulty, such as you 'tick' for those of moderate difficulty and two 'ticks' for the harder ones. This way, you'll know which questions to concentrate on as you move around the circle to get a second and third time. Using this technique could also provide you with the opportunity to take your breaks once you have finished each circle.

As soon as you have finished your three circles, you may find that you have a few questions remaining and are proving especially difficult. Depending upon how much time you've left, try to fix these concerns as best you can, or at least take a rough guess. Remember, there's absolutely no negative marking in the CISSP exam.

THE SPECIFIC TERMS OF CISSP, THE MOST COMMONLY USED TERMS AND THEIR MEANING

Term - Definition

Acceptable risk

A suitable level of risk commensurate with the possible advantages of the business's operations as determined by senior management.

Access control system

Means to ensure that access to assets is licensed and limited according to business and security requirements related to logical and physical systems.

Access control tokens

The system determines if access is to be granted or denied based upon the validity of the token for the point at which it is read based on date, time, day, holiday, or other condition used for restraining validation.

Accountability

Accountability ensures that account direction Has assurance that only authorized users are accessing the machine and using it properly.

ActiveX Data Objects (ADO)

A Microsoft high-level interface for all types of data.

Address Resolution Protocol (ARP)

It can be used in the Media Access Control (MAC) Layer to provide for direct communication between two devices in precisely the exact same LAN segment.

Algorithm

A mathematical function that's used at the encryption and decryption processes.

Asset
A product perceived as having worth.

Asset lifecycle

The stages an advantage goes through from creation (collection) to destruction.

Asymmetric

Not identical on each side. In cryptography, key pairs are used, one to encrypt, the other to decrypt.

Attack surface

Different safety testing systems find distinct vulnerability types.

Attribute-based access control (ABAC)

This can be an access management paradigm whereby access rights are granted to users with policies that combine attributes together.

Audit/auditing

The tools, processes, and activities used to perform compliance reviews.

Authorization

The procedure of specifying the specific resources a User needs and determining the type of accessibility to these resources the user might have.

Availability

Ensuring timely and reliable access to and usage of Info by authorized users.

Baselines

A minimum level of safety.

Bit

Most crucial representation of information (zero or 1) at Layer 1 of the Open Systems Interconnection (OSI) model.

Black-box testing

Testing where no internal details of the system Implementation are used.

Bluetooth (Wireless Personal Area Network IEEE 802.15)

Bluetooth wireless technology is also an open standard for short-range radio frequency communication used chiefly to set wireless personal area networks (WPANs), and it's been integrated into several kinds of business and consumer devices.

Bridges

Layer 2 devices that filter traffic between Segments based on Media Access Control (MAC) Addresses.

Business continuity (BC)

Actions, processes, and resources for ensuring a company can continue critical operations during a contingency.

Business continuity and disaster recovery (BCDR)

A word used to collectively describe company continuity and disaster recovery efforts.

Business impact analysis (BIA)

A list of the company's assets annotated to reflect the criticality of each asset to your organization.

Capability Maturity Model for Software or Software Capability Maturity Model (CMM or SW-CMM)

The maturity model focused on quality management procedures and has five maturity levels which contain several key practices in each maturity level.

Cellular Network

A radio network spread over land areas called cells, each served by a minimum of one fixed-location transceiver, known as a cell site or base station.

Certificate authority (CA)

An entity trusted by one or more users as an authority which issues, revokes, and manages digital certificates to bind individuals and entities to their public keys.

Change direction

A formal, methodical, comprehensive procedure for requesting, reviewing, and approving changes to the baseline of their IT environment.

CIA/AIC Triad

Security model with the three security concepts of confidentiality, integrity, and availability make up the CIA triad. It is also sometimes known as the AIC Triad.

Ciphertext

The modified form of a plaintext message, in order to be unreadable for anyone except the intended recipients. One thing that has been turned into a secret.

Classification

Arrangement of assets into classes.

Code-division multiple access (CDMA)

Every call's information is encrypted with a unique key, then the calls are all sent simultaneously.

Common Object Request Broker Architecture (CORBA)

A set of standards that Addresses the requirement for Interoperability between hardware and software solutions.

Compliance

Adherence to a mandate; the activities displaying adherence along with the tools, processes, and documentation that are used in adherence.

Computer virus

A program written with purpose and functions to replicate and distribute itself without the knowledge and collaboration of the owner or user of their computer.

Concentrators

Multiplex connected devices into a single sign to be transmitted on a network.

Condition coverage

This standard requires adequate test cases for each requirement in a program decided to take on all possible outcomes at least once. It differs from branch coverage only when multiple states must be assessed to reach a determination.

Confidentiality

Preserving authorized restrictions on information access and disclosure, including means for protecting personal privacy and proprietary information.

Configuration management (CM)

A formal, methodical, comprehensive procedure for setting a baseline of the IT environment (and each of the resources within that environment).

Confusion

Offered by mixing (shifting)the Critical values used during the repeated rounds of encryption. When the key is modified for every round, it provides added complexity that the attacker would encounter.

Content Distribution Network (CDN)

It is a large distributed system of servers installed in multiple data centres throughout the world wide web.

Covert channel

An information flow that is not controlled by a security management and has the chance of disclosing confidential details.

Covert security testing

Performed to mimic the threats that are Related to external adversaries. While the safety team has no knowledge of the covert test, the organization management is fully aware and consents to the test.

Crossover Error Rate (CER)

This is accomplished when the type I and type II are equal.

Cryptanalysis

The study of methods for obtaining the meaning of encrypted information without having access to the secret information that is usually required to make the purchase.

Cryptography

Secret writing. Today provides the ability to reach confidentiality, integrity, authenticity, non-repudiation, and access management.

Cryptology

The science which deals with hidden, concealed, or encoded information and communications.

Curie Temperature

The critical stage where a substance's intrinsic magnetic orientation changes management.

Custodian

Responsible for protecting the advantage that has value, whilst in the custodian's possession.

Data classification

Entails assessing the data that the organization retains, ascertaining its importance and value, and then assigning it to a class.

Data custodian

The person/role inside the business owner/controller.

Data flow coverage

This criterion requires sufficient test intervals for each feasible data flow to be executed at least one time.

Data mining

A decision-making technique that is based on a string of analytical techniques taken from the fields of math, data, cybernetics, and genetics.

Data owner/ control

An entity that collects or generates PII.

Data subject

The individual human-related to a set of private data.

Database Management System (DBMS)

A suite of application programs that typically manages large, structured sets of persistent data.

Database model

Describes the connection between the information Components and provides a framework for organizing the information.

Decision (branch) coverage

Considered to be a minimum level of coverage for Most software products, but decision coverage alone is inadequate for high-integrity software.

Decryption

The inverse procedure from encryption. It's the Process of converting a ciphertext message back into plaintext via using the cryptographic algorithm and the appropriate key which was used to perform the initial encryption.

Defensible destruction

Eliminating data using a controlled, legally defensible, and regulatory compliant way.

DevOps

A strategy based on lean and agile principles in which company owners and the development, operations, and quality assurance departments collaborate.

Diffusion

Provided by mixing up the location of the plaintext through the ciphertext. The strongest algorithms exhibit a high degree of confusion and diffusion.

Digital certification

An electronic document that Includes the title of a company or individual, the business address, the electronic signature of the certificate authority issuing the certificate, the certificate holder's public key, a serial number, and the expiry date. Used to bind entities and individuals to their public keys. Issued by a trusted third party referred to as a Certificate Authority (CA).

Digital rights management (DRM)

A Broad Selection of technologies that grant control and security to content suppliers above their own digital media. May use cryptography techniques.

Digital signatures

Give authentication of a sender and integrity of a sender's message and non-repudiation services.

Disaster recovery (DR)

These tasks and actions needed to bring an organization back from contingency operations and reinstate normal operations.

Discretionary access control (DAC)

The machine owner decides who gets access.

Due care

A legal concept concerning the duty owed by a Provider to a client.

Due diligence

Actions are taken by a vendor to demonstrate/provide because of care.

Dynamic or Private Ports

Ports 49152 -- 65535. Every Time service is asked that is connected with well-known or registered ports these solutions will respond using a dynamic interface.

Dynamic testing

When the system under test is executed and its behaviour is observed.

Encoding

The action of changing a message into another format by using a code.

Encryption

The process of converting the message from the plaintext into cipher text.

False Acceptance Rate (Type II)

This is incorrect recognition by perplexing one user with another, or by accepting an imposter as a valid user.

False Rejection Rate (Type I)

This can be a failure to recognize a valid user.

Fibre Channel over Ethernet (FCOE)

A lightweight encapsulation protocol and it lacks the reliable data transfer of the TCP layer.

Firewalls

Devices that enforce administrative safety Policies by filtering incoming traffic according to a set of rules.

Global System for Mobiles (GSM)

Each call is transformed into digital data which is given a channel and a time slot.

Governance

The procedure of how a company is managed; usually includes all elements of how decisions are made for that organization, such as policies, functions, and procedures the organization uses to make those choices.

Governance committee

A formal body of personnel who decide how Decisions will be created inside the business and the thing that could approve exceptions and changes to current relevant governance.

Guidelines

Suggested expectations and practices of action To best achieve tasks and attain goals.

Hash function

Accepts input of any length and generates, via a one-way functionality, a fixed-length output called a message digest or hash.

Honeypots/ honeynets

Machines that exist on the community, but don't contain sensitive or valuable data, and therefore are meant to distract and occupy malicious or unauthorized intruders, as a way of delaying their efforts to access production data/assets. Some of the machines of this kind, connected together as a network or subnet, are referred to as a "honeynet."

Identity as support (IDAAS)

Cloud-based services that broker identity and Access Management (IAM) functions to target systems on customers' premises and/or in the cloud.

Identity proofing

The process of collecting and verifying information about a person with the aim of demonstrating that a person who has asked an account, a credential, or other particular privilege is really who he or she claims to be and establishing a trusted connection that may be trusted electronically between the individual and said credential for functions of digital authentication.

Initialization vector (IV)

A non-secret binary vector used since the initializing Input algorithm, or a random starting point, for the security of a plaintext block arrangement to boost security by introducing additional cryptographic variance and to synchronize cryptographic equipment.

Integrated Process and Product Development (IPPD)

A management technique that simultaneously integrates all essential acquisition activities through the use of multidisciplinary teams to improve the design, manufacturing, and supportability processes.

Integrity

Guarding against improper information modification or destruction and includes ensuring information non-repudiation and authenticity.

Intellectual property

Intangible assets (especially contains applications and data).

Internet Control Message Protocol (ICMP)

It provides a means to send error messages and also a way to probe the network to determine network availability.

Internet Group Management Protocol (IGMP)

Used to manage multicasting groups that is a set of hosts anywhere on a system which are listening for a transmission.

Internet Protocol (IPv4)

It is the dominant protocol that operates in the Open Systems Interconnection (OSI) Network Layer 3. IP is responsible for addressing packets so that they may be transmitted from the origin to the destination hosts.

Internet Protocol (IPv6)

Is a modernization of IPv4 that includes a much bigger address area: IPv6 Addresses are 128 bits that encourage 2128 hosts?

Intrusion detection system (IDS)

An option that monitors the environment and automatically recognizes malicious efforts to gain unauthorized access.

Intrusion prevention system (IPS)

A solution that monitors the surroundings and automatically takes action once it recognizes malicious efforts to gain unauthorized access.

Inventory

Complete collection of items.

Job rotation

The practice of getting personnel to become comfortable with numerous positions within the organization as a means to reduce single points of failure and also to better discover insider threats.

Key Clustering

When different encryption keys generate the same Cipher text from precisely the same plaintext message.

Key Length

The size of a key, typically measured in bits, that a cryptographic algorithm uses in ciphering or deciphering safe info.

Essential or Crypto variable

The input that regulates the operation of this cryptographic algorithm. It determines the behaviour of the algorithm and enables the dependable encryption and decryption of the message.

Knowledge Discovery in Databases (KDD)

A mathematical, statistical, and visualization method of identifying legitimate and useful patterns in data.

Least privilege

The practice of only granting a user the minimum permissions necessary to execute their explicit job role.

Lifecycle

Phases an advantage goes through from production to destruction.

Log

A record of events and actions that have taken place on a computer program.

Logical access control system

Non-physical system which allows access based upon pre-determined policies.

Loop policy

This standard requires sufficient test cases for all application loops to be implemented for zero, one, two, and lots of iterations covering initialization, typical running, and termination (boundary) conditions.

Mandatory access controls (MAC)

Access management that requires the system to manage access controls in accordance with the company's security policies.

Maximum allowable downtime (MAD)

The measure of how long a company can endure an interruption of critical functions. Also known as maximum tolerable downtime (MTD).

Media

Any item which contains data.

Message authentication code (MAC)

A small block of data that is generated with a secret key and then appended to the message, used to deal with integrity.

Message digest

A small representation of a larger message. Message digests are used to make sure the authentication and integrity of data, not confidentiality.

Metadata

Information about the data.

Misuse instance

A use case in the perspective of an actor hostile to the system under design.

Multi-condition coverage

These standards require sufficient test cases to Exercise all possible combinations of conditions in a program choice.

Multi-factor authentication

Ensures a user is that he or she claims to be. The more variables used to ascertain an individual's individuality, the greater the trust of credibility.

Multiprotocol Label Switching (MPLS)

Is a wide area networking protocol that works at both Layer 2 and 3 and does label switching?

Need-to-know

Primarily associated with organizations that assign clearance levels to all users and classification amounts to all resources; limits users with the same clearance level from sharing data unless they are working on the exact same effort. Entails compartmentalization.

Negative testing

This ensures the application can gracefully handle invalid input or unexpected consumer behaviour.

Network Function Virtualization (NFV)

The objective of NFV would be to decouple functions such as firewall management, intrusion detection, network address translation, or name service resolution from specific hardware implementation into software solutions.

Non-repudiation

Inability to deny. In cryptography, a service that ensures the sender can't deny that a message was sent and the integrity of this message is undamaged, and the receiver can't assert receiving another message.

Null cipher

Hiding plaintext within another plaintext. A form of steganography.

Open Authorization (OAUTH)

The OAuth 2.0 authorization framework enables a third-party application to obtain limited access to an HTTP service, either on behalf of a resource owner by orchestrating an approval interaction between the resource owner and the HTTP service, or by allowing the third-party application to obtain access on its own behalf.

Open Shortest Path First (OSPF)

An interior gateway routing protocol developed for IP networks based on the shortest path first or link-state algorithm.

OSI Layer 1

Physical layer.

OSI Layer 2

Data-link layer.

OSI Layer 3

Network layer.

OSI Layer 4

Transport layer.

OSI Layer 5

Session layer.

OSI Layer 6

Presentation layer.

OSI Layer 7

Application layer.

Overt security testing

Overt testing can be used with both internal and external testing. When used from an internal perspective, the bad actor simulated is an employee of the organization. The organization's IT staff is made aware of the testing and can assist the assessor in limiting the impact of the test by providing specific guidelines for the test scope and parameters.

Ownership

Possessing something, usually of value.

Packet

Representation of data at Layer 3 of the Open Systems Interconnection (OSI) model.

Packet Loss

A technique called Packet Loss Concealment (PLC) is used in VoIP communications to mask the effect of dropped packets.

Parity bits

RAID technique; the logical mechanism used to mark striped data; allows recovery of the missing drive(s) by pulling data from adjacent drives.

Patch

An update/fix for an IT asset.

Path coverage

These criteria require sufficient test cases for each feasible path, basis path, etc., from start to exit of a defined program segment, to be executed at least once.

Personally, identifiable information (PII)

Any data about a human being that could be used to identify that person.

Physical access control system

The term Physical Access Control System defines a physical system that prevents unauthorized entry into protected or dangerous areas, while still guaranteeing access to those who are regularly authorized.

Ping of Death

Exceeds maximum packet size and causes the receiving system to fail.

Ping Scanning

Network mapping technique to detect if the host replies to a ping, then the attacker knows that a host exists at that address.

Plaintext

The message in its natural format has not been turned into a secret.

Point-to-Point Protocol (PPP)

It provides a standard method for transporting multiprotocol datagram over point-to-point links.

Policy

Documents published and promulgated by senior management dictating and describing the organization's strategic goals.

Port Address Translation (PAT)

An extension to NAT to translate all Addresses to one routable IP address and translate the source port number in the packet to a unique value.

Positive testing

This determines that your application works as expected.

Privacy

The right of a human individual to control the distribution of information about him- or herself.

Procedures

Explicit, repeatable activities to accomplish a specific task. Procedures can address one-time or infrequent actions or common, regular occurrences.

Purging

The removal of sensitive data from a system or storage device with the intent that the data cannot be reconstructed by any known technique.

Qualitative

Measuring something without using numbers, using adjectives, scales, and grades, etc.

Quantitative

Using numbers to measure something, usually monetary values.

Real user monitoring (RUM)

An approach to web monitoring that aims to capture and analyze every transaction of every user of a website or application.

Recovery point objective (RPO)

A measure of how much data the organization can lose before the organization is no longer viable.

Recovery time objective (RTO)

The target time set for recovering from any interruption.

Registered Ports

Ports 1024 – 49151. These ports typically accompany non-system applications associated with vendors and developers.

Registration authority (RA)

This performs certificate registration services on behalf of a Certificate Authority (CA).

Remanence

Residual magnetism left behind.

Residual risk

The risk remaining after security controls have been put in place as a means of risk mitigation.

Resources

Assets of an organization that can be used effectively.

Responsibility

The obligation of doing something. It can be delegated.

Risk

The possibility of damage or harm and the likelihood that damage or harm will be realized.

Risk acceptance

Determining that the potential benefits of a business function outweigh the possible risk impact/likelihood and performing that business function with no other action.

Risk avoidance

Determining that the impact and/or likelihood of a specific risk is too great to be offset by the potential benefits and not performing a certain business function because of that determination.

Risk mitigation

Putting security controls in place to attenuate the possible impact and/or likelihood of a specific risk.

Risk transference

Paying an external party to accept the financial impact of a given risk.

Role-based access control (RBAC)

An access control model that bases the access control authorizations on the roles (or functions) that the user is assigned within an organization.

Rule-based access control (RBAC)

An access control model that is based on a list of predefined rules that determine what accesses should be granted.

Sandbox

An isolated test environment that simulates the production environment but will not affect production components/data.

Security Assertion Mark-up Language 2.0 (SAML 2.0)

A version of the SAML standard for exchanging authentication and authorization data between security domains.

Security control framework

A notional construct outlining the organization's approach to security, including a list of specific security processes, procedures, and solutions used by the organization.

Security governance

The entirety of the policies, roles, and processes the organization uses to make security decisions in an organization.

Segment

Data representation at Layer 4 of the Open Systems Interconnection (OSI) model.

Separation of duties

The practice of ensuring that no organizational process can be completed by a single person; forces collusion as a means to reduce insider threats.

Session Initiation Protocol (SIP)

It is designed to manage multimedia connections.

Time multiplexing

Allows the operating system to provide a well-defined and structured access to processes that need to use resources according to a controlled and tightly managed schedule.

Time of check time of use (TOCTOU) Attacks

Takes advantage of the dependency on the timing of events that takes place in a multitasking operating system.

Transmission Control Protocol (TCP)

Provides connection-oriented data management and reliable data transfer.

Transport Control Protocol/ Internet Protocol (TCP/IP) Model

The layering model structured into four layers (network interface layer, internet layer, transport layer, host-to-host transport layer, application layer).

Transposition

The process of reordering the plaintext to hide the message by using the same letters orbits.

Trusted computing base (TCB)

The collection of all of the hardware, software, and firmware within a computer system that contains all elements of the system responsible for supporting the security policy and the isolation of objects.

Trusted Platform Module (TPM)

A secure crypto processor and storage module.

Uninterruptible power supplies (UPS)

Batteries that provide temporary, immediate power during times when utility service is interrupted.

Use cases

Abstract episodes of interaction between a system and its environment.

User Datagram Protocol (UDP)

The User Datagram Protocol provides connectionless data transfer without error detection and correction.

Virtual Local Area Networks (VLANs)

Allow network administrators to use switches to create software-based LAN segments that can be defined based on factors other than a physical location.

Voice over Internet Protocol (VoIP)

It is a technology that allows you to make voice calls using a broadband internet connection instead of a regular (or analog) phone line.

Waterfall Development Methodology

A development model in which each phase contains a list of activities that must be performed and documented before the next phase begins.

Well-Known Port

The term indicates the most common port numbers that are between 0 and 1023 (0 to 210 - 1). They are used in system processes that provide network services.

White-box testing

A design that allows one to peek inside the "box" and focuses specifically on using internal knowledge of the software to guide the selection of test data.

White listing/ blacklisting

A white list is a list of email Addresses and/or internet Addresses that someone knows as "good" senders. A blacklist is a corresponding list of known "bad" senders.

Wi-Fi (Wireless LAN IEEE 802.11x)

Primarily associated with computer networking, Wi-Fi uses the IEEE 802.11x specification to create a wireless local-area network either public or private.

WiMAX (Broadband Wireless Access IEEE 802.16)

One well-known example of wireless broadband is WiMAX. WiMAX can potentially deliver data rates of more than 30 megabits per second.

Work factor

This represents the time and effort required to break a cryptography system.

TIPS AND TRICKS TO PASS THE EXAM

Studying with the ultimate goal of passing the CISSP is like all those tasks that are considered difficult.

1. It should be treated as a long run and not a sprint. The amount of material to be studied is large and the guide is made up of about 1,400 pages. It must be divided into sections and you should not move on to the next section until we are sure that you have mastered the section studied.

2. A stimulating deadline must be established but must be achievable by the date on which the exam will take place. Before starting you need to have significant training.

3. The test is not necessarily "real life." In many cases, more than one answer is right. The question is generally asked to find the best answer. Take as many practice tests as you can. Quizlet is a good app. (ISC)2 also provides plenty of resources.

4. Study using your most successful learning style, but add a few others. I learn best by writing, which I did while reading, watching and listening to the materials.

5. Lean on the domains in which you are weaker, you must strengthen them by concentrating on them.

6. Train a lot when you are close to the test data. There is nothing like a concentrated final push to prepare and strengthen your security. When you take

the training camp, get ready. You must increase concentration in the days preceding the exam by eliminating all possible distractions.

7. Try to get enough sleep and rest in the days leading up to the exam.

8. If studying is like a race, so is the exam itself

9. (You must try to isolate the best answers from the red herring.) So, read the question very well and remember that the process tends to isolate the two best choices.

10. Be in the moment for each question. Your confidence will be tested. Some questions will appear from nowhere. Some don't even count as they are being tested for future exams. You won't know which is which. Do your best on a question, answer it and then forget it. The only question that matters is the one you're on.

HOW TO APPROACH DIFFICULT CISSP EXAM QUESTIONS

The first thing most people think after what they are told about the CISSP exam is how difficult the questions are. While this can be a good helper, it doesn't help prepare you for the exam. Knowing the facts isn't enough for some of the CISSP exam questions. These questions are nicknamed "difficult questions". In this section, we will look at seven types of difficult questions you might find in the CISSP exam and the best approaches to solving them.

Most of the CISSP exam will put your knowledge of these aspects in serious difficulty. However, remember that mere knowledge of these aspects does not prepare you for facing the most difficult questions you may see on the CISSP exam. An important and significant part of the course is reserved for study skills, the best memorization techniques, the correct application of concepts and principles. Although it is impossible to guess exactly which questions will be found during the exam, we can classify difficult questions into seven categories and provide examples and approaches to identify and overcome them.

1.1 Detailed knowledge questions

Description

These questions require detailed knowledge of a technology or principle.

Example

At what level of the OSI model can a bit-level packet be corrected?

a) Level 2
b) Level 3
c) Level 4
d) Level 5

Reply

The correct answer is a) Level 2. is the data link level. Specifically, Media Access Control is a level 2 sub level that performs error checking. If a single bit is wrong, it can mark it as an error or, in case we have a parity bit, it can rebuild the frame and perform a bit-level error correction. Level 4 (transport) also checks for errors, but is based on a package. If a level 4 error is detected, it can only request a retransmission. This is just a difficult question.

Approach
Study well and try to reflect on the question. it is still necessary to know the safety-relevant aspects of mechanisms and techniques, even if CISSP is commonly described as "a mile wide and an inch deep". There are several approaches to comparing and contrasting similar and alternative mechanisms. For example, error correction can be performed at level 2, level 4 and even level 7.
You have to ask yourself what is the difference between error correction at levels 2, 4 and 7. Also, you need to make sure you understand the difference between the four DES output modes. For example, why would anyone use ECB over CBC?

1.2 Questions about the subset

Description

These are questions where at least two of the answers are correct but one is clearer than the others. Many of these questions can be viewed as a subset question where one or more of the answers are actually subsets of the correct answer.

Example

An attack involving an attacker creates a misleading context for the purpose of inducing a user to make a bad security decision is known as:

a) Spoofing attack
b) surveillance attack
c) social engineering attack
d) Man-in-the-middle attack

Reply
The correct answer is c) Social engineering attack. Both a) and c) imply misleading, but only social engineering involves contact with the user (social) and leads to a wrong security decision (engineering).

Approach
First, it must be recognized as a subset question. It is useful to draw arrows from one answer to another if you think that the first answer is a subset of the second. So we have to ask ourselves if the "inner" answer is always correct or not. If the response of the subset is always correct, we choose that. If not, we choose the one that is correct

1.3 Too many information questions

Description

This is a type of question that gives you too much information. Often the candidate is tricked into finding an appropriate equation to use all the variables offered in the application.

Example

When carrying out a risk assessment, the following values are developed for a specific threat / risk pair. Asset value = 100 K, exposure factor = 35%; The annual occurrence rate is 5 times a year; the cost of recommended protection is $ 5000 per year, which will reduce the hope of annual loss by half. What is SLI?

a) $ 175,000
b) $ 35,000
c) $ 82,500
d) $ 77,500

Reply
The correct answer is
b) $ 35,000. SLE is simply AV x EF.
a) it is ALE;
c) the ALE improvement given that the safeguard was put in place;
d) is the safeguard value.

CISSP TOPICS AND RESOURCES

The demand for credible and qualified security professionals is increasing with the increasing sophistication of hackers and cyber criminals. The International Information Security Certification Consortium o (ISC)² is an organization that offers cutting-edge certifications in the field of information security. Their flagship CISSP is one of the main certifications that can help a security professional to stand out from the competition by acquiring the best skills in the sector. So have you decided to get the honor of being a CISSP certification holder? Do you want to know how to proceed with the training? Which topics require the most attention and which can be overlooked with less importance? Planning an examination of CISSP's stature can be a difficult task; therefore, in this section, we will share the most important CISSP resources (that every candidate should know.

THE BOOKS

While studying for CISSP, you should try to gather as much reading material as you can. Here is a list of books that we think you should read if you want to complete your preparation:

Official (ISC)² Guide to CISSP CBK, Fourth Edition [(ISC)² Press]

The list does not follow a particular order but let's start with the best: the official guide (ISC)². This book is the only official preparation guide you'll find on the market. The administration made changes to the CBK in 2015 and this book includes all those changes.

All the 8 domains (Security and Risk Management, Asset Security, Security Engineering, Communications, and Network Security, Identity and Access Management, Security Assessment and Testing, Security Operations and Software Development Security) are comprehensively covered in the book. The book's content has been endorsed and approved by many practitioners and experts from all over the world.

In addition to the good things though, there are some drawbacks to the book as well:

It is not formatted professionally. The recently released edition has serious design flaws including missing pages, monotonous content, and language errors, etc.
The book is sometimes too verbose for an applicant's liking. This describes the absence of literacy skills in the author.

All in all, the book may have verbosity problems and may give problems with its poor formatting, but it is still one of the most beautiful pieces of CISSP
CISSP Study Guide

The study guide written by Seth Mishear, Eric Conrad and Joshua Feldman is a brilliantly written book that is extremely popular with aspirants.

Over 600 pages long, the book is much shorter than the competition, to begin with. Seth, Eric, and Joshua are connoisseurs in the field of information security and their intuition and experience have allowed them to create a highly reliable book for candidates for preparation. The book is very complete and not intimidating at all. It is not detailed and does not needlessly deepen the technical concepts.

However, not everyone believes that being short is the soul of wit; many aspirants are of the view that the book does not fully understand all the topics and during the preparation, they also use other guides. The book was recently updated to include changes made to the CBK in 2015.

CISSP: Certified Information Systems Security Professional Study Guide (Sybex)

This book has been authored by Mike Chapple, Darril Gibson, and James Stewart jointly. For those aspirants that are just trying to start their preparation, this book is the optimal choice.

TheSyrex guide's latest edition incorporates the updates made in 2015; the book encompasses all the CISSP bulletin objectives of 2015 (Application development security, disaster recovery planning, cryptography, and access control, etc.) When you buy the package, you get unprecedented access to the online learning environment set up by Syrex, which includes:

- Searchable key-term glossary.
- An interactive test simulating engine.
- More than 1400 practice questions.
- More than 1000 electronic flashcards.
- An extensive guide to help you prepare for the CISSP certification.

The book has 1080 pages and can give you a great head-start in your bid to prepare comprehensively for the CISSP.

CISSP Cert Guide

Robin Abernathy and Troy McMillan are 2 IT certification experts and their book, the CISSP Cert Guide is as simple as a guide to the CISSP exams.

The book is written in a very simple way to understand and explains personal, cryptographic and operational security issues in a complete and detailed way. However, the book does not actually cover all the domains, so it is not advisable to consider it as the only exam preparation resource but to integrate with other guides. You can get the book here.

CISSP for Dummies

Lawrence C. Miller wrote this book as part of the for dummies series. The book is easy to read and provides applicants with access to the test engine and online portal. However, the book has not been updated since 2012.

ONLINE RESOURCES

Sampliner's resource library

The resources available on the Sampliner website have high-quality articles, tests to practice, video clips and e-books that can be considered useful by aspiring CISSPs. To access the repository you don't need any registration and you can browse it to explore it.

The CISSP Sunflower study guide

The CISSP Sunflower study guide is a concise and neatly organized collection of study cards that help you prepare for the CISSP exam. The cards are divided into categories according to the domain and each section describes the topics which are explained under the given headings. The "Things to know" summaries available at the end of the sections make the guide much more advantageous.

The free test on Yasna.com

Many aspirants perform free sample tests.

INFOSEC

The INFOSEC Institute also offers free CISSP training and a study guide that has been found incredibly beneficial by candidates over the years.

5. Community Reddit

There is a widespread community on Reddit where CISSP experts and aspirants interact with each other to find, among other things, answers to intriguing questions. you can publish a post with the necessary questions to clarify your doubts.

YOUTUBE VIDEO GUIDE

There are many certified professionals who have made full videos to help aspirants with their preparations.

Ports 0 to 1023 ports are related to the common protocols used in the underlying management of the TCP / IP (Transport Control Protocol / Internet Protocol) system, Domain Name Service (DNS), Simple Mail Transfer Protocol (SMTP), etc.

It involves the use of only one of the three factors available exclusively to perform the required authentication process.

It involves the use of only one of the three factors available exclusively to perform the required authentication process.

An automated system that manages the passage of people or goods through an opening in a secure perimeter based on a series of authorization rules.

PRACTICE EXAM RESOURCES

There Are Lots of practice exam resources on the market the world wide web and from the industry too. Some of the very worth-mentioning ones are:

> CISSP practice examinations (2nd edition)

The CISSP practice exams is a Superb booklet That covers most of the ten of those (older) domains which (ISC)² used to possess from the CBK. It supplies aspirants having the capability to boost their training by trying practice evaluations. Approximately 1000 queries are offered on the internet portal site, the access to that will be allowed to individuals who buy the publication. The publication also offers 30 hours of sound training by the writer, Shon Harris. On the other hand, the book has not been updated following the modifications that were made in 2015.

Skillset.com

Skillset is a test prep Test engine with a few of the key highlights for example.

- Countless CISSP test explanations and questions -- free for everybody.
- A certificate readiness score so you'll understand when you are prepared to take the examination
- A breakdown of questions by topic area
- EXAM PASS GUARANTEE (with PRO membership)

CISSP Exam Prep Questions, Answers & Explanations: 1000+ CISSP Practice Questions with Thorough Solutions

SSI Logic also printed a publication that attempts to provide the aspirants with an array of practice tests to examine their training. You will find over 1000 queries and about 19 condensed mock examinations offered from the publication. The publication's ultimate purpose is to boost the aspirants' preparations to this extent that they're ready to clear their examination in their first attempt. The publication has also been upgraded following the CBK changes created in 2015.

The publication, however, is a source for you to find clinic tests in and may only be advantageous when it is used along with a broader textbook. Additionally, many aspirants and specialists have claimed that a few of the questions covered in the publication are beyond the scope of the CISSP CBK.

Boson

The Three clinic CISSP examinations (everyone has 250 questions) accessible at Boson price 40 bucks each. But we urge (according to public view) that examinations no. 3 and 2 will be the only ones worth carrying; do not take the examination no. 1.

CCCURE

If you are a devout CISSP aspirant then you have to Have learned about CCCURE by today; however in case you have not, then it is really your blessed day. CCCURE is a bookmarking site for everyone the CISSP candidates. There are hundreds and hundreds of practice questions and tools available which may be considered crucial. The quiz portal site on the web site lets you pick the difficulty level of their practice questions together with the CBK resources which you need them to be from.

Cram sessions at Quizlet.com:

You will find lots of cram sessions available in Quizlet which may help you a good deal during your prep. These sessions are usually accompanied by evaluations and/or practice examinations.

Printed in Great Britain
by Amazon